CULTURE SHOCK!

Japan

P. Sean Bramble

Graphic Arts Center Publishing Company
Portland, Oregon

In the same series

Argentina	*Ecuador*	*Laos*	*South Africa*
Australia	*Egypt*	*Malaysia*	*Spain*
Austria	*Finland*	*Mauritius*	*Sri Lanka*
Belgium	*France*	*Mexico*	*Sweden*
Bolivia	*Germany*	*Morocco*	*Switzerland*
Borneo	*Greece*	*Myanmar*	*Syria*
Brazil	*Hong Kong*	*Nepal*	*Taiwan*
Britain	*Hungary*	*Netherlands*	*Thailand*
California	*India*	*New Zealand*	*Turkey*
Canada	*Indonesia*	*Norway*	*UAE*
Chile	*Iran*	*Pakistan*	*Ukraine*
China	*Ireland*	*Philippines*	*USA*
Costa Rica	*Israel*	*Portugal*	*USA—The South*
Cuba	*Italy*	*Saudi Arabia*	*Venezuela*
Czech Republic	*Japan*	*Scotland*	*Vietnam*
Denmark	*Korea*	*Singapore*	

Barcelona At Your Door	*Paris At Your Door*	*A Student's Guide*
Beijing At Your Door	*Rome At Your Door*	*A Traveller's Medical Guide*
Chicago At Your Door	*San Francisco At Your Door*	*A Wife's Guide*
Havana At Your Door	*Shanghai At Your Door*	*Living and Working Abroad*
Jakarta At Your Door	*Tokyo At Your Door*	*Personal Protection At Home & Abroad*
Kuala Lumpur, Malaysia At Your Door	*Vancouver At Your Door*	*Working Holidays Abroad*
London At Your Door		
Moscow At Your Door	*A Globe-Trotter's Guide*	
Munich At Your Door	*A Parent's Guide*	
New York At Your Door		

Illustrations by TRIGG

Front cover photograph by P. Sean Bramble
Back cover photograph by Japan National Tourist Organization
Inside photographs by P. Sean Bramble, except for photograph on page 137 by Japan National Tourist Organization

© 2004 Marshall Cavendish International (Asia) Private Limited

This book is published by special
arrangement with Marshall Cavendish International (Asia) Pte Ltd
Times Centre, 1 New Industrial Road, Singapore 536196
International Standard Book Number 1-55868-852-8
Library of Congress Catalog Number 2004-111396
Graphic Arts Center Publishing Company
P.O. Box 10306 • Portland, Oregon 97296-0306 • (503) 226-2402

Printed in Singapore

*This book is affectionately dedicated to
my beautiful daughter
Hana Joyce
who is as much a newcomer to Japan as
most all of my readers*

CONTENTS

iv

INTRODUCTION

Whap! That's the sound as you slap your forehead and exclaim, "My goodness – I'm really in Japan!" I did it when I first got to Japan years ago and, you know, I still do it from time to time. There are so many things about Japan that are completely at odds with whatever you've experienced in your home country, such as dinner entrees that are still moving or company meetings that aren't. Even now I sometimes still get that funny feeling that something is culturally amiss, something I just can't put my finger on. That feeling is culture shock, of course.

Fortunately, most every newcomer to Japan manages to get some good advice from an "old hand" in how to cope with the country. In my case that old hand was Phil Swann, a prematurely balding, extremely funny Brit. He would politely nod as I told him about the latest culture clash I'd endured, and then in a very kindly tone of voice he'd say, "Japan is certainly an unbelievable country, isn't it? Let's go have a beer." I cannot say whether it was Phil's outstanding advice that got me through those rough early days, or if it was simply the Kirin lager, but in any case I progressed quite neatly along the up-and-down, love/hate curve of cultural adjustment to Japan.

So it is that I have felt tremendous responsibility in writing this book for those newcomers (that's *you*!) who are contemplating a trip here. Partly that is because of the huge cultural differences one must obviously overcome, but mostly because I've noticed there are too many self-serving publications put out about Japan, endlessly nattering on about how absolutely marvy it all is here. Japan is neither paradise nor inferno; it's just what you make of it.

My hope, with this book, is to point you in the right direction and help you over the inevitable humps. And if you find you still have any questions left unanswered, come find me at the local *izakaya*, pull up a stool, and call out, *"Awa o sukunaku shite kudasai!"* ("Just a small head on the beer, please!") It's the first Japanese phrase I learned from Phil.

ACKNOWLEDGMENTS

I suppose I could have written this book without interviewing another soul, but then I wouldn't have found it to be particularly interesting, plus I would have had no one else to tell my bad jokes to. Instead, I found it much more fun to talk with a lot of other people, drink some coffee or beer, and actually learn something new. To everyone who helped I would like to say that it was a lot of fun, especially the second round.

Thanks go to lots of people, starting with my lovely wife, Junko, who did a marvelous job of pretending to understand all of the self-inflicted agonies that writing brings out in me, and an even better job of supporting me in any way she possibly could.

I would also like to thank my parents, who didn't kick up too much of a fuss the day I told them I'd decided to head off to Asia; this book is a happy by-product of their understanding.

Also deserving of kudos are Mark Elliott, who thoughtfully remembered me from Lower Nowherestan and suggested I write this book, and my ever-patient editor, Yumi Ng. Particularly generous with their time and assistance were, in alphabetical order, Shogo Asaji, Robert Bennett, Timothy G. Breitkreuz, Funaki Kyouko, Harada Hideo, Hirano Emiko, Ikko Mayumi, Katsuta Sachiko, Kibe Mayuko, Karen Kluttz, Koga Chikako, Michael C. Kontas, Kouzuru Dai, Clinton J. Lambourn, Duncan G.R. Lawrence, Fred Lyle, Matsumoto Maki, Scott Newby, Nishitani Kaoru, Greg O'Keefe, Saeki Tomoko, Dr. Ronald Schlemper, Elliott J. Schuchardt, Sugi Tomoko, Dr. Takao Mami, Tanaka Miwa, Moses Yamane, and Yoshida Yuuko.

Finally, I would like to thank the hundreds of my students who, over the years, have kindly explained many of the remarkable intricacies of Japanese society and culture to me. Any mistakes that might be lurking within this tome are, as Robert Plant would sing, nobody's fault but mine.

Note on the Romanization of Japanese Words

If some of the Japanese words in this book look a little different from the way they are written elsewhere, there is a good reason for this!

Elongated vowels in Japanese present a small problem when written in Roman letters, because of many people's initial tendency to pronounce the vowels as they appear in English. For example, *chou* (町, meaning town) does not rhyme with "ouch" but rather with "oh", and *ookii* (大きい, meaning big) does not sound like "uki" but instead like "oh-ki". Many books about Japan in the English language render all elongated vowels as a single letter, usually "o" or "u", with a macron above it (*chō, chū*), or they stick in a letter "h" after it (*choh*).

A problem, however, arises when you take your first steps in learning the language. I found this out when I spent an hour inputting "Tokyo" into my new electronic Japanese/English dictionary in an attempt to learn the kanji for the city, and all I got was an error message. (A little cartoon professor would appear and say, "You schmuck! Don't you know how to spell in Japanese?") It took a kind co-worker to teach me that "Tokyo," written as the Japanese pronounce it, should actually be spelled *Toukyou*. Ever since, whenever I see a new Japanese word in Roman letters with an "o" in it, I end up wondering if the "o" is actually "oo" (おお), or "ou" (おう), or merely "o" (お).

With my editor's gracious agreement, and with our faith in our readers' ability to quickly grasp this key point in Japanese pronunciation, we have decided to present Japanese words in Roman letters that more nearly approximate their Japanese spelling. There are some words, notably place names, that are beyond fixing ("Osaka" should really be spelled *Oosaka*), but most all other words have been diligently transcribed in what we think is a much more sensible way. All Japanese words in this book appear in italics. We hope that you find our rendering of Japanese to be helpful in the long run.

If not, I fully expect the cartoon professor to pay me another visit.

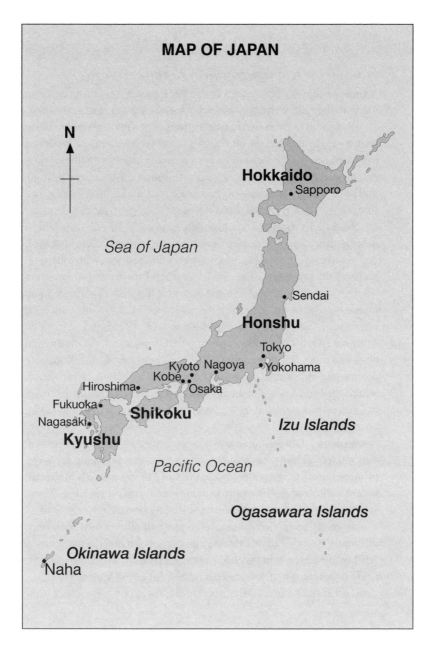

MAP OF JAPAN

N

Hokkaido
Sapporo

Sea of Japan

Sendai

Honshu

Tokyo
Kyoto Nagoya
Kobe Yokohama
Hiroshima Osaka
Fukuoka
Nagasaki Shikoku
Kyushu

Izu Islands

Pacific Ocean

Ogasawara Islands

Okinawa Islands
Naha

Chapter One

THE LAND AND ITS PEOPLE

"History is a set of lies agreed upon."

–Napoleon

GEOGRAPHY

Japan is a collection of islands that lies at the northeastern margin of Asia. Comprising four major islands—Honshu, Hokkaido, Kyushu, and Shikoku— and about 1,000 smaller ones, it stretches in a gentle east-west arc from a latitude equivalent to the tip of Maine to that of Key West. The climate ranges from temperate to subtropical—and, as one might expect, it can run the gamut of fierce weather. Winters in Hokkaido and the Tohoku region can be brutal, June is officially rainy season, and the best that can be said about summer is that it is hot and humid—just wait till the typhoons blow through!

MOUNT DOOM: *Volcanoes, like this one in Kagoshima, are popular tourist attractions.*

Topographically, Japan is mostly mountainous, with a few large plains but almost no major rivers to speak of. As part of the Pacific Ocean's "ring of fire", it has many volcanoes (some dormant like Mount Fuji; some active like Sakurajima). It is also prone to earthquakes, and seaside areas sometimes experience impending danger from the accompanying tsunamis.

Most of the mountains—at least the ones that haven't been bulldozed in the name of "development"—are covered with a variety of domestic and foreign deciduous and evergreen tree species, including pine and cedar. Many lowland areas are still devoted to the tilling of rice, but many of the rice fields that once lay within city limits have since been converted to apartment blocks. Japan also has some beautiful flowers that make their appearance throughout the warmer months.

There is very little wildlife dangerous to man; Japanese wolves became extinct a century ago, and bears outside Hokkaido are hard to find. There are snakes, but even the *habu* snakes of Okinawa are not as poisonous or deadly as snakes of the world go. In fact, the most dangerous creature you might run across is the *mukade*, an evil-looking centipede that leaves a nasty welt if it bites you. Otherwise, the most prominent animals seem to be spiders, insects of all kinds (including butterflies and dragonflies), birds (crows, cranes, kites, ducks, and seagulls), clever monkeys, obnoxious deer, and urban rats.

POLITICAL GEOGRAPHY

Today, Japan is administratively divided into 47 prefectures called *ken*; thus, Chiba Prefecture is *Chiba-ken* in Japanese. A few places within the administrative divisions, however, are not technically classified as prefectures, such as Tokyo-to, Osaka-fu, Kyoto-fu, and Hokkaido.

Each prefecture is further divided into either cities (*shi*) or counties (*gun*). Within counties or smaller cities there are further divisions of towns (*chou* or *machi*); larger cities are often first divided into wards (*ku*) and then into smaller subdivisions. Addresses are written the reverse of how they are written in Western countries, with the postal code coming first, followed usually by prefecture, city, subdivision, neighborhood, block, building, apartment number, and finally, addressee's name. Though some streets may have names, most do not, which means finding a particular address can be a real chore even for Japanese, let alone travelers from another country.

There is only one time zone for Japan, and there is no daylight savings time. Enjoy the June sunrise on your face at 5 a.m.

HISTORY

Japanese history is fascinating, and since much of it lies outside the purview of history courses in the West, here's a brief overview of it.

3

Early Culture

Where the Japanese came from, no one can say with any anthropological authority. Some hold that the Japanese are distantly related to the Mongoloid peoples of Central Asia, others say that the Japanese have connections to either the people of Southeast Asia or Polynesia. Regardless, it seems likely that over time there was a fusing of peoples and cultures from disparate points of the Pacific Rim. The earliest of Japan's ancient peoples was the Joumon, a nomadic people with roots dating to the Middle Stone Age (10,000–3,000 B.C.) They were followed by the Yayoi (300 B.C.–A.D. 300), a stone and metal age people who practiced rice cultivation, advanced pottery techniques, and the manufacture of iron and bronze implements.

Japanese legend holds that Ninigi, grandson of the Sun Goddess, touched down to Earth near Ebino in Kyushu. His grandson, Jimmu, became in 660 B.C. Japan's first emperor, striking forth from Kyushu and eventually settling near Osaka. Archaeologists, however, doubt

CHESSBOARD: *Rural communities are still a patchwork of fields growing rice and other crops.*

both the date and the absurd longevity attributed to the early emperors; it is more likely that Japan was conquered in a similar direction by the Yamato state around A.D. 400.

Learning From China

As a small island nation located on the periphery of a great empire, it was Japan's fate to be heavily influenced by China. During the early years of those contacts, China was already one of the great empires of the world, while Japan's civilization was just beginning to grow. In those early years, travelers and official delegations went back and forth between the two countries, bringing to Japan the Buddhist religion, Chinese technology, and the Chinese calendar.

Chinese influence in Japan was momentous, and is still undoubtedly greater than many Japanese might care to admit. It's not just the enduring capacity of Chinese lettering (*kanji*), of which Japan is the only non-Chinese country to have continued with this system. It's also felt in the cuisine, arts, and sorrowful history shared by the two countries. Even today, in the technology-charged 21st century, there remains, at the same time, a strong sense of mutual admiration and simultaneous mistrust between the two countries, an unpleasant dynamic that may never get resolved. The story goes that China feels it taught Japan everything it ever learned; Japan retorts that that was hundreds of years ago, and China hasn't learned anything new since. That symbiosis, of the proud teacher and the impatient student, would make itself felt in this corner of the world time and again.

Civil Wars

We skip ahead a few centuries to find the Japanese engaged in a protracted series of bloody civil wars. If, after serious study, you find yourself confused by the different alliances and personalities involved, don't feel bad. Ordinary Japanese have the same difficulty keeping things straight.

5

Basically, all you need to know is that, following the Heian period (794–1185), in which classical Japanese arts flourished, the country entered a period of upheaval dominated by aspiring leaders and their families. The year 1185 is significant, because that is the year that the warrior leader Minamoto no Yoritomo basically ignored Emperor Go-Toba and established his own military government in Kamakura. He eventually was recognized as *shougun*, or preeminent military leader, by the emperor, but the intrigue of that particular era was just starting to get under way. By 1333, Japan seemed to be in perpetual conflict, as noble families and courts changed sides in a constant struggle for advantage. Betrayal and violence were the order of the day, and the violence was quite bloody indeed. Beyond the conflicts between political aspirants, there were also clashes between classes, as peasants rose up and revolted against oppressive lords.

One of the legendary events of Japan occurred during this time, as the Mongol leader Kublai Khan attempted an invasion of Japan in 1274. A great storm arose, however, and many Mongol ships were destroyed and the invaders drowned. Seven years later the Mongols attempted a second invasion, and again a "divine wind" (*kamikaze*) destroyed the Mongols' invasion fleet.

A complicating factor during the latter stages of Japan's civil wars was the arrival of Europeans to Kyushu. The Spanish and the Portuguese, and later the Dutch, began trading with the Japanese, most notably at Nagasaki. They brought with them firearms and the Christian religion. Eminently practical, the Japanese rejected the religion but kept the weapons. Though many peasants and not a few lords converted to Christianity, in the end, the *shougun* Tokugawa Ieyasu decided that the religion was a threat to his power and had it forcefully suppressed. That, combined with the concurrent expulsion of foreigners and the virtual cessation of trade with the West, meant that Japan had entered the period of near-total isolation known as the Tokugawa Shogunate.

Tokugawa Japan

With Tokugawa and his descendants in charge, Japan entered the Edo Period. Over a period of a few centuries, real power—if not its trappings—slowly ebbed away from Japan's military rulers and toward its commercial classes. This was a time of expansion in the visual, literary, and dramatic arts, as well as increased urbanization. However, the tight control exerted by the *shougun* over the populace kept Japan politically frozen. Although some thoughtful Japanese advocated a more open approach to the world, they argued their points very softly—to do so loudly risked their lives.

Then, in 1853, U.S. Commodore Matthew C. Perry, under instructions from President Millard Fillmore, arrived in Edo Bay in his famous "black ships" with instructions to open Japan to trade. The next 15 years saw the Tokugawa Shogunate totter and, unable to defend the country from better-armed foreigners, collapse. Reforming Japanese rallied around the young emperor Meiji and used the imperial line as a focal point to change the country and make it strong enough to resist the West. Japan's modern age had begun.

Meiji Restoration

During the reign of Meiji, Japan underwent an astonishingly turbulent period, as the nation's leaders decided that Japan had to abandon the traditions of hundreds of years and instead emulate the Western powers that were extending domination over Asia. Feudalism was abolished, a national military was created, railroads were built, and a constitution was written. Political parties mushroomed but were kept from overturning the government's applecart, and financial leaders asserted strong control over an overheating economy by pursuing a policy of deflation.

Internationally, Japan achieved victory against China on the battlefield in the 1890s, but lost it at the negotiating table when Western countries united to limit Japan's territorial gains. That war was followed by the Russo–Japanese War of 1904–1905, in which

Japan astonished the world by defeating a Western power. (The war notably began when Japan launched a surprise attack on the Russian base at Port Arthur, a move which was widely praised for its audacity by at least one English newspaper.) One result of that war was Japan's annexation of Korea in 1910.

Taisho Democracy

The 1920s and early 1930s are known as the period of "Taisho Democracy", named after the emperor whose reign was vaguely concurrent. During this time career opportunities started to open up for women, young people began marrying as they wished, and Western fashions and modes of entertainment began to filter down into the lives of regular people. But the increased consumerism and ostentatiousness were displeasing to many, and as Japan became frustrated due to other countries' protective immigration and economic measures, right-wing groups began to assert stronger control. A series of prime ministers and other liberal leaders were assassinated, and the military assumed greater control over the civilian government. The country became obsessed with expanding, and as it looked around the world, it could only see shadowy enemies who seemed ready to deny Japan its rightful place in the world.

World War II

In 1931, Japan attacked China and established its own puppet state in Manchuria called *Manchuukuo*. Then, in 1937, the war with China escalated after Japanese troops clashed with a Chinese garrison at the Marco Polo Bridge, near Beijing. In the ensuing conflict, the Japanese army proved itself to be an effective fighting force, but with China's seemingly infinite manpower and territory Japan could not bring things to a conclusion. More ominously for Japan, the U.S. expressed strong support for China, and began to deny Japan the raw materials it needed to continue its expansion. Faced with an America hostile to its goals, Japan in 1941 launched a series of attacks upon Manila,

SACRIFICED: *A museum displays photos of the young kamikaze pilots who flew to their deaths in World War II.*

Malaya, Singapore, Hong Kong, Guam, Wake, and of course Pearl Harbor in Hawaii. All were successful, many of them suddenly so.

That first rush was about as good as Japan was going to experience during the war. Though Japan eventually consolidated its gains by securing the Philippines, it proved unable to progress beyond those initial gains. Eventually, the Allies counterattacked, avoiding strong points by island-hopping where practicable, and engaging in deadly, close-range jungle fighting where it wasn't. By 1945 the Allies were bombing Japan on an almost daily basis.

Surrender was finally being considered by Japan's civilian authorities. The problem was that it wasn't being considered by its military leaders. Having resolutely gambled on a risky war, and having seen their bullheaded, unimaginative strategy trumped time and again by the Allies, the generals and admirals found themselves boxed in by pride. They absolutely refused to capitulate. To that point they had already sacrificed millions of lives in their struggle for

9

national supremacy, but they announced that Japan would not be defeated until the Allies had slaughtered the entire population. "The deaths of 100 million would be glorious," they trumpeted.

Emperor Hirohito had supported the earlier phases of the war, either because of the heady promise of early successes or by letting himself be intimidated by older men supposedly under his command. But in the closing days of the war he finally listened to the voices of his suffering people. Finding his government deadlocked on the issue of surrender, he broke with tradition and gave his own opinion to the government, saying that the country should give up immediately. His recorded announcement was broadcast to the nation on 15 August 1945; he asked the nation to "bear the unbearable" and accept defeat. Some accepted harder than others. Even though surrender had the imprimatur of the emperor himself, a good many military officers were prepared to thwart the imperial will and planned to launch one more surprise attack on the arriving Allies. Only extremely strenuous pleas from other members of the imperial family managed to suppress these plans and prevent the resumption of even-more vengeful fighting.

Occupation

Even before the Allied armies had even stepped foot in Japan, a completely unarmed General MacArthur had stepped off his airplane and settled into quarters in Tokyo. Thus began the Occupation of Japan which, while ostensibly an effort to be managed by all of the victorious Allies, became essentially an American project. Determined to remake Japan as a more democratic society, MacArthur broke up the prewar industrial combines, instituted a major land reform, and personally wrote Japan's postwar constitution. That last item is controversial to this day as it contains the famous Article 9, which forever renounces Japan's right to wage war.

Economically devastated by war, Japan had to begin all over again, with very little to start with apart from a very determined and talented work force. Politically, Japan was swinging to and fro in the postwar years, in part because the developing Cold War was affecting U.S. plans for its defeated enemy. In the beginning, women's rights were dramatically improved, labor unions were supported, and a peaceful, egalitarian society seemed in the making. But very quickly the U.S. became less concerned about Japan's ability to attack its neighbors and more concerned about Japan's ability to support the U.S. military in the Far East. With its tacit blessing, the conservative business establishment began to wrest control of the government away from the left, and has kept it ever since.

Economic Phoenix

As soon as the Occupation ended, Japan set about running things as it saw best. Freed from the financial burden of providing for its own defense, Japan was able to focus solely on economic growth. Other equally valid demands were shunted aside. Those they couldn't ignore, the leaders did their best to slow down. National pride lay solely in rising GNP, and the Japanese worker willingly complied in

Ho-hum: *Tall towers, rows of cars, pedestrians everywhere–in other words, an unremarkable day in Tokyo.*

11

doing anything it took to help Japan get ahead. By the 1960s, Japan's cameras, cars, and motorcycles were starting to seize market share abroad; by the 1970s, those shares dramatically expanded and were joined by an expansion in shipbuilding, electronics, and durable goods. Competing industries in other countries were staggered by the Japanese invasion, and many of them either shrank or disappeared entirely. By the end of the 1970s, Japan was being proclaimed as No. 1. It was the beginning of endless trade friction with the West.

Both European and American negotiators proved unable to halt Japan's economic barrage. First, Japan began to establish even more manufacturing operations abroad, thereby avoiding the issue of exporting from Japan altogether. Second, Japanese companies that earned money abroad refrained from converting that money back into yen, thus avoiding putting even more upward pressure on an ever-stronger currency.

But even though some appreciation of the yen was unavoidable, increasing the purchasing power of Japan, a funny thing happened: Japan learned that it loved being rich. Coupled with a simultaneous easing of credit by the Bank of Japan, people found that they had all the money they needed to buy whatever they wanted. And, oh, did they buy!

Before, Japan had always sent a few select people abroad to study the ways of the competition. Now the country could easily afford to bring foreign experts to Japan in whatever number was deemed necessary. A boom in designer goods unfolded, as people developed a hunger for the finer things in life, whether bags or clothes or foods or cars. Abroad, Japanese began traveling in growing numbers. Merchants in other countries learned they could get rich merely by catering to Japanese tourists. Nor were Japanese companies immune from the frenzy. They bought a famous building here and a movie studio there, and they plowed so much money into building golf courses abroad that the environmental degradation was shocking.

The value of property in Japan, on which so much domestic

borrowing depended, grew and grew until it reached absurd proportions all out of touch with reality. At one point the value of the land upon which the imperial palace rested in the heart of Tokyo was equivalent to, say, Canada (although one shudders to think how much wrapping paper Japan would use to bag that particular purchase!) Meanwhile, the stock market, unburdened with paying dividends to shareholders, soared until in 1989 it touched a stock average of 38,915.87. Euphoria was in the air; Japan *was* No. 1.

All that you need to understand subsequent events is one figure: In October 2002, the Nikkei stock average slipped below 8,200. By such a measure, nearly 80 percent of its wealth had evaporated.

Japan in Malaise

With the deflation of the bubble, Japan saw its economy tumble into a near-permanent state of recession. Exactly what are the reasons it did so are difficult to pin down, but there are some obvious markers. The yen rapidly appreciated until in 1995 it briefly touched 80 yen for one U.S. dollar, throttling Japan's export industry in its tracks. A number of Japanese investments abroad went sour, and other companies suddenly realized that, deluded by the easy credit of the 1980s, they had grossly overpaid for too many shiny baubles. Other countries in Asia, particularly the slumbering giant known as China, began to follow Japan's economic model and, because of lower costs, outperformed their teacher. Japanese management practices, so widely touted a decade previously, were suddenly perceived as being too unwieldy and cost-heavy. A shrinking birthrate began to imperil the tax base, and an expanding number of senior citizens put added pressure on a burdened health system. Deficit spending, already bloated by far too many environmentally damaging construction projects, soared to 150 percent of GDP because political leaders were incapable of making difficult choices. The ballooning public debt turned Japan's credit rating into one of the shakiest in the world. And on and on.

While obviously not as ravaging as a full-fledged depression, there were signs that Japan's years of endless recession were taking their toll on the people at large. University graduates found themselves without work and dependent on their parents. Businesses confessed that the lifetime employment scheme was really a charade after all; workers had loyally kept their end of the bargain, but companies in turn did everything they legally could to restructure employees out of their positions. Household incomes dropped, and families turned to loan sharks in a desperate and sometimes fatal attempt to keep themselves going. The number of crimes increased, and the number of suicides spiked. And pervading all of this was a particularly Japanese sense of gloom that things were just not going to get any better no matter what.

Although there were signs that the recession was ending at last, there were also enough worries that, economically speaking, Japan was in an absolute pickle and unable to extract itself from its predicament. Argentina's monetary crisis was often cited as a parallel for Japan. The difference was that Japan's effect on the world economy so dwarfed Argentina's that any economic catastrophe centered in Japan might engulf the world as well. In that case, it was possible that not even the full faith and credit of the U.S. government, often cited as the last resort for such a disaster, would have been enough to prop up the international financial system.

Japan was belatedly coping with too many holes in the dike at the same time, and though other countries insisted on Japan making faster changes, those countries of course backed off if the expected result was total collapse. Japan, in short, was the country too big to fail. But sometimes things that aren't supposed to fail do so anyway.

GOVERNMENT AND POLITICS

Japan today is a parliamentary democracy. The parliament, known as the Diet, has two chambers. The upper house is the House of Councillors, or *Sangi-in*; the lower house is the House of Representa-

Big election: *Wooden boards with candidates' posters appear as election season gets under way. It's a good time to buy earplugs.*

tives, or *Shuugi-in*. As in Britain, the lower house is the stronger of the two. Elections must be held for each house at intervals of no more than four years. There is also an allegedly independent court system, with a 15-member Supreme Court at its head.

The head of government is the prime minister, who is usually the leader of the largest political party. He appoints the heads of various ministries that collectively make up his cabinet. As a practical matter, however, the most powerful man in each cabinet department is the minister's deputy, who is the department's highest-ranking civil servant. Japan's legendary bureaucracy is notoriously difficult for any political leader to control, and many bureaucrats take the liberty of "suggesting" legislation to the political leaders who are in a position to authorize it.

Political power is supposed to be shared between the national government and the separate regional governments; however, since the national government holds some very lucrative purse strings, it is able to influence economic development around the country. Yet there are also times when the national government seems politically

15

unable or unwilling to step into local matters, even urgent ones. A spectacular example would be the government's thoroughly inept response in the immediate aftermath of the Kobe earthquake in early 1995. How many died because of bureaucratic delays and infighting while organizing the rescue of survivors is not a matter of pleasant speculation.

Politics

Japan's primary ruling political party for most of the postwar period has been the Liberal Democratic Party which, as one wag suggested, doesn't seem to be particularly liberal, or democratic, or even much of a party. Philosophically, they picked up where the prewar business leaders left off, and certainly the 1930s party members were liberal for their time, considering that the alternative was the clique of militarists.

For 38 years without interruption (1955–1993), the LDP ruled Japan. The party appealed to conservative businessmen and farmers and worked the political system to the benefit of both. The party was, like all large political parties in Japan today, less a monolithic force than a collection of factions (*habatsu*) which competed with each other for power. As there is nothing fairer in Japan than to let the qualified and unqualified alike have a turn, that's how each faction was able to push its own candidate for prime minister.

Early in postwar Japan the country had a vigorous opposition in the Socialist Party. For a few years they did hold power, but as economic benefits continued to trickle down the longer the LDP stayed in power, the Socialists slipped into second-class status: always ready to attack the government, but never able to persuade a majority of voters that they should be entrusted with the machinery of government.

The Communist Party, unable to have great effect on national decisions, nevertheless has a lot of sympathy in many quarters. Since the end of the Cold War its power has even waxed in some years, as many people see the party as being the one group willing to take an uncompromising stand against the rampant corruption that has engulfed the LDP.

The rumblings of discontent over the years, as well as the LDP's own fossilization, contributed to its loss of power in the lower house elections of 1993. A coalition of opposition parties gravitated around one party called Sakigake and selected one of its leaders, former LDP member Hosokawa Morihiro, as prime minister. However, calls for change bogged down because, although the LDP was out of power, individual LDP members still held great sway over the bureaucracy. Many top-level bureaucrats had grown comfortable working with the LDP and did what they could to brake reform.

Coupled with the inherent difficulties of such a wide-ranging coalition being able to agree on anything, the LDP was able to slip back into power the following year—by making a Faustian bargain with its prior enemy, the Socialist Party! This bizarre creation lasted until the LDP was able to reassert sole power in a subsequent election. Since then, the Socialist Party, tarnished as a group of turncoats blinded by power, has since limped away into general irrelevance.

The LDP's main opposition today comes from the Democratic Party of Japan. The party has built itself over successive elections to become the focus of anti-LDP resentment, although policy differences between the two parties are not always readily apparent. The party does have an image of clean government because of its founder Kan Naoto, who as health minister in 1996 forced the government to admit its complicity in distributing blood products tainted with HIV.

Today, the LDP has gerrymandered itself into a surviving relic of the Cold War. It continues to take tax monies from urban workers and pork barrels it out to the rural residents, who in return continue to solidly back the LDP. Its leaders are often clueless about the legislation that is arranged in their names. Moreover, the principle of "one man, one vote" does not really apply in Japan. Votes in the countryside continue to be weighted more heavily in comparison to those of city dwellers, who are more likely to support the LDP's opponents. Yet Japan's Supreme Court has refused to take charge of the situation, saying that it merely hopes the legislators will recognize the problem and rectify it at some future date.

The Imperial Family

In the background of Japanese politics stands the imperial family. It is said to be the longest-lived dynasty of all the world's royal leaders, but much of that longevity is possibly due to the fact that it has remained curiously irrelevant through much of Japan's history. During the shogunate, the emperor was more or less a prisoner in Kyoto. When the imperial family was restored to prominence, the emperor was essentially co-opted into establishing an aura of legitimacy to the new leadership of Japan. Today, although considered the head of state, the imperial family since 1946 has no connection whatsoever with the machinery of government.

The current emperor is Akihito, and his reign is known in Japan as *Heisei*. In public Akihito seems like a genial, unassuming man. His wife, Michiko, was the first empress not to have been born to aristocracy; she and the emperor famously met while playing tennis. They make appearances at only the most innocuous of public events: meeting schoolchildren, planting rice, or presiding over public functions. The family's periodic outings are planned by the Imperial Household Agency, a small organization which is alleged to hold great power over what each family member does and says.

Akihito's eldest son, Naruhito, is married to Princess Masako, a beautiful and brilliant former employee of Japan's foreign ministry. There was speculation upon their 1993 marriage that she would become an outspoken humanitarian in the mold of Princess Diana, and many people were disappointed that she has mostly disappeared from public view. But even if Masako-sama has been subsumed into the cloistered world of the imperial family, it seems that change will undoubtedly come to this institution as well. Apart from Naruhito and his younger brother, all of the other possible inheritors to the imperial title are female. In today's Japan, there is no provision for the imperial title to be passed on to a woman, and this is an uncomfortable development for many.

In conversation, many ordinary Japanese will express their indifference or even hostility to the idea of an imperial family. However, it is impossible to find an example in Japanese media of either criticism or ridicule of the institution along the sort of lines that the British royal family endures. While it is possible that the majority of the Japanese would be accepting of such treatment, the question is moot since the broadcasters and publishers are unwilling to cross that line.

Chapter Two

THE JAPANESE

"Better to die than to live in shame."

–Japanese proverb

Picture this: A print of Edo-period Japan, exquisitely drawn with fine lines and soft colors. In a peaceful moment one sees cranes posed in mid-stride, budding cherry blossoms, and fragile maidens holding parasols. The image suggests quiet and tranquility and *stasis*—the sense that matters have been frozen in time forever, because change cannot overcome this scene at all.

Today, the cranes have had their habitats destroyed, the trees have had their limbs lopped off, and the young women wear miniskirts and jabber loudly with their friends. But that image of Japan and of the average Japanese, heroically impervious to any outside pressure, persists. One look at the typical salaried worker, his face passive to events around him, and you would be forgiven if you thought he was meditating in some Zen-like way. Self-disciplined, dutiful ... what an absolute portrayal of serenity he exudes.

It ain't exactly that way, however. Though the average Japanese is astonishingly self-disciplined and dutiful, it is fatuous to suggest that he is serene. On the contrary, he is at the epicenter of a number of conflicting pressures. From 180 different points on his right side he is buffeted by 180 obligations, and from 180 opposite points on his left side he is battered by an equal number of antinomous duties. He has responsibilities to people within his group that conflict with those to people outside his group. He must behave toward his seniors in a way that is completely different from how he treats his juniors. He must forever keep a lock on his emotions, yet he feels as strongly as any other human being on this planet. Pinned into the center of this compass of competing strains, he is not so much serene as he is trapped, much like he is trapped everyday onto an impossibly crowded subway car, unable to even scratch his nose.

If everyone in Japan is not cut out for this—and it is clear that many are not—it is nevertheless a powerful statement on the strength of the human will that a good number of Japanese can endure these rigors and still lead productive, happy lives.

THE PRESSURES OF HARMONY

By far the greatest task that each Japanese person faces is the need to maintain harmony within the group. Known as *wa*, it is the widespread belief that people should keep good relations with everyone so that there are only good feelings all round. If there are differences of opinion between two people, then they should do what they can to smooth over those differences. If one person is at odds with everyone else in the group, then it is up to that one person to do what he can to restore a harmonious relationship.

Given that there are billions of people on this planet with billions of opinions on every subject, it seems unrealistic to say the least to expect everyone in a certain group to feel exactly the same way regarding everything. One might argue (as I often do) that harmony comes from a healthy ability to tolerate and respect differences among people. The Japanese do have tremendous toleration for those people outside whatever their group is at the particular moment, it is true, but within their group there is great expectation that everyone will think and do as everyone else. That expectation is vaguely narcissistic, it's probably unhealthy, it's certainly monotonous — it's Japan.

The desire for *wa* does not only trump individual opinions regarding, say, a serious matter such as a particular company's future direction. It manifests itself in the smallest ways as well. I know a woman who would periodically go out for dinner with her colleagues. After a moment of looking at the menu, the senior-most woman would choose what she wanted for dinner — and everyone else would just coincidentally choose the same meal as well. Except this one woman. She would choose something different, something that she wanted to eat, and for the rest of the meal she would have to listen to tiny comments made by the others. "She usually likes to order something different, doesn't she?" "She must be a very unique person." "Wow, how does your dinner taste?" And so on.

As you have probably figured out by now, a lot of the pressure to maintain harmony comes from the fact that others in one's group are complicit in enforcing harmony. Those who suppress their own individuality are free from abuse. Those who insist on thinking and doing as they like must constantly endure the petty tyrannies of the group.

There is a saying in Japan that goes, "The nail that sticks up gets hammered down." (Since this saying is guaranteed to appear in every other book explaining the country's society, I would like to propose a corollary: "The hoary Japan cliché that is put away gets trotted out again.") It goes a long way to explaining why no one wants to be different. No one wants to get hammered time and again. And it also means that those who do stand up and express themselves are very brave individuals indeed. Either that, or just a bit odd.

Pressures Up and Down

Like other Asians, Japanese customarily show respect for their superiors, and expect as much from their inferiors. Within the family, children address their mothers as *okaasan* and their fathers as *otousan*; it's a bit like calling one's parents "Mrs. Mom" and "Mr. Dad". At school, students go along with rules laid out by upperclassmen. The fact that some people may truly find their parents or school-mates unworthy of respect is irrelevant. The very form of respect, whether genuine or artificial, is necessary to maintain a harmonious relationship.

This perpetual division of people into two groups, one older than oneself and the other younger, carries over to the office. One never has

SHOW SOME RESPECT. *Junior employees still pour drinks for senior ones at company parties.*

colleagues *per se* in a Japanese office; one's co-workers are either seniors (*sempai*) or juniors (*kouhai*). Seniors are almost always older both in actual age and in terms of service to the company—those two factors inevitably go hand in hand—while juniors aren't. Even for co-workers who are the same age and were hired at exactly the same time, the tiniest gradation can still exist—whoever has the earlier birthday is technically the senior person.

Many psychologists have studied this interdependence between older and younger people in society and have found patterns similar to the "parent-child" relationship known as *oyabun-kobun*. In this scenario, the older person (a parent, a boss, a teacher) must establish a strict atmosphere to accomplish whatever is the task at hand, but there must also be occasional intervals in which he demonstrates his indulgence and allows the younger person time to cavort or complain. In turn, the younger person must show complete respect, as well as unlimited endurance in doing what the older person asks of him.

In its most extreme form, this becomes abusive and/or violent, as senior people will treat their juniors very badly indeed. I saw a young music teacher break down into tears because she had had a slight fender-bender, and the school principal made her apologize at a school meeting to every teacher for her horrible transgression. She then had to write a thorough report for him describing what she had done and how she would improve herself in the future. People in charge make painful examples of those who commit the smallest of offenses.

Pressures In and Out

Certainly there are many hierarchical elements in Japan that can be found throughout Asia: respect for one's ancestors (particularly the dead), a tradition of children supporting their parents when they get older, and the importance of continuing the family name. What is most surprising, however, is how companies can trump the obligations normally rendered to one's family. Companies demand, and

routinely receive, a fealty from their workers that would be unimaginable almost anywhere else. They can do this because of the shifting curtains between "in" and "out" known as *uchi* and *soto*.

In its basic form, *uchi* refers to a family and denotes those members who are part of the family. *Soto* means those who are outside the family. Within the family one can show emotion and argue; in front of outsiders, however, one must smile and show that "everything's great"; to do otherwise would be a tremendous embarrassment. Moreover, this pattern of in-and-out relationships is carried over to other groups, demarcating the line between host and guest, Japanese and non-Japanese, Toyota employees and Nissan employees, even between departments within a company.

Of course there are times when the two duties conflict; does one attend the graduation of one's child, or go to work as always? In Japan, feudalism still reigns and the company is held in higher esteem than the family. Ninety-five percent of family members watching a child's graduation are female.

This division between in and out exists in parallel form with regards to people's feelings. *Tatemae* are the words that people express in public; *honne* are the words that express people's true feelings. It often requires a thorough acquaintance with a Japanese person before you can be satisfied you have correctly understood his or her feelings on an important matter—you have to be trusted as an insider. Generally speaking, younger people are more open than older ones, and women more so than men.

The Pressure of Keeping Face

Face is an important concept in Asia, and Japan is no exception. No man likes to admit he was wrong in front of his subordinates, and no one wants to be shown up by a competitor. A lot of men (and women too) have an inability to confess mistakes and will continue to plow ahead to the point of complete destruction. Of course there's no one in life who likes to say he screwed up, but in Japan it definitely seems to be taken to extremes.

It is very important when dealing with Japanese people that, even if you are 100 percent right and the other is 100 percent wrong, you find a way for the other party to gracefully claim some honor while conceding. Do not demonstrate your total superiority and rub your opponent's nose in it. It makes great sense to behave magnanimously since it is quite possible that your paths will cross again. If you act imperiously, however, you will only engender resentment and, as one writer has noted, few things pervade Japan's literature through the centuries so much as themes of revenge.

Pressures of Duty and Feeling

Two concepts that are forever at war with each other are duty (*giri*) and human feelings (*ninjou*). The average Japanese lives in a world in which, from the moment he wakes up until the time he goes to bed, he is drowning in duty: to his spouse, to his boss, to his colleagues, to his club, to his community, to his country. Since all of those groups have a multitude of rules, and since it would be shameful to be exposed as being weak and unable to meet the requirements of any

PARTY ON. *Many dinner parties look like this: long tables, communal plates of food, and lots of conversation.*

one of them, many people will simply exhaust themselves trying to keep up with them all. Obviously, it can be simply overwhelming to please everyone, and in fact not a few people crack because they feel their responsibilities so deeply that they are literally unable to function.

Which is why, when a person in a superior position steps forward to show compassion for an inferior's situation and perhaps bend the rules a bit, the lower-ranking person is positively grateful. To be relieved of his burden, however fleetingly, is all that many people ask in life. As it stands, though, some people will try to avoid all of their responsibilities if given the chance. The result is that conservatives will argue that Japan should return to an old-time ethic of bone-crushing duty because that's all that will keep people in line.

The Pressure to Be Social
It's hard to get away in Japan. The average working Japanese has to spend long hours in close proximity with his co-workers every day.

He has to spend his nights drinking with people he may not really care for. He is crammed into trains with everyone else. Life is a succession of lines and crowds and commitments to others, all of which must be borne with good grace.

Understandably, there is a limit as to how much people can stand. So in public people sort of turn off. They don't notice things around them if they don't have to; many times I've met a friend on the street and had to frantically shout and wave just to get his attention. He wasn't ignoring me—he was just a million miles away.

In fact, Japanese are so sensitive to this wish to escape from others that they will sense it even when it's not there. Six weeks after my friend Shiho's wedding, I called her best friend and asked how Shiho was doing. Her best friend said she didn't know because she was sure the new bride just wanted to be left alone. Surprised, I then called Shiho. "I'm so glad you called," she said. "No one has called me since I got married. I feel bored."

The Pressure to Do Something Now

Great religions and moral codes arise as a reaction to a culture's excesses. If Zen, with its emphasis on meditation and inner peace, was able to reach full flower in Japan, it is probably because Japanese life is full of duties that must be attended to immediately, if not sooner. "Could I borrow your stapler?" I casually asked my colleague. She yanked her desk drawer open, grabbed the stapler, and *ran around* the desks to hand it to me. There have been so many mornings that I've walked through the door to work and been instantly confronted with documents that needed signing or plans that needed changing. "Um, could you at least wait until I take off my jacket?" I ask.

I've had guests from abroad who say they've never seen people walk in as much of a hurry as they do in Japan. And these comments are from people who've been to New York City.

EMOTIONS IN AND OUT OF PLAY

To many, overt displays of emotion are seen as shameful. That does not mean that some people don't yearn for affection the same as anyone else; they do. One student told me that the most romantic thing she could imagine was to be kissed in public; her boyfriend, however, was too shy to even contemplate so doing.

Which is maybe why, when people do get emotional, they go the whole hog. Weddings bring forth copious tears from the bride as she gives her thank-you speech; it's expected. Students at school graduations (and the PTA chairwoman) weep just as much; the ceremony is not a fist-pumping achievement but the heart-breaking dissolution of the group. Most embarrassingly, Japanese Olympic athletes famously start bawling for the TV cameras whenever they lose or win. C'mon, guys—buck up!

The same applies to anger; when a Japanese man gets angry, he goes berserk. Perhaps he does so partly because he hopes the magnitude of his tirade will be intimidating in and of itself. I saw a port office absolutely rocked by the screaming vulgarities of a *yakuza*, who blistered the staff because he'd arrived five minutes too late to get his car onto the ferry. To their credit, the port officials stood their ground, but I couldn't help but notice how they had massed behind the poor guy who'd initially taken the abuse. Stern-looking,

WAIL! I'M SO HAPPY!!!

with their arms crossed, their poses seemed to say they would defuse the situation simply by absorbing all of his emotional energy into their unemotional ranks.

The rule seems to be that emotions are the weapon of last resort — that such a blatant expression of feeling must truly show one cares, which in turn makes one right and the other party wrong. Still, if one looks through the emotion, one can see the absurdity of many lachrymose spectacles. I remember a scene years ago, when a Japanese man had declared he was on a hunger strike to protest some outrage or other, and his family was on TV tearfully imploring the government to change its policy before he wasted away and died.

At that stage the man had been on his hunger strike for four hours.

Maturity—What a Concept!

One thing that immediately strikes you about Japan is that there's an awful lot of cuteness going on. Young adults will drive cars that have lots of cute stuffed animals piled up on the dashboard. College students will practice wheelies on their bicycles on college campuses. Middle-aged office workers will while away their empty hours reading comic books. What is going on here?

If it seems that some people in Western countries wish they could be 17 again, then it seems Japanese wish they could be about seven. Many Japanese will, to the Western eye, act emotionally rather than reasonably. This is seen as an admirable trait in Japan; to many, logic is the tool of the cold-hearted, and persuasive words are for the serpent-tongued. Better instead to be a child,

Peko-chan, the girl with the bobbying head, is a familiar advertisement for a cake company.

with all the wide-eyed innocence and purity that childhood denotes, rather than to be an adult with its concomitant drudgery and responsibility. The merchandise that people buy and the way in which they act merely reflect that attitude.

CLEAN AND DIRTY

Paging Dr. Freud! What is it that makes people wash stone and concrete, or take forever in the bath? Partly it's explained by Shinto's emphasis on ritual washing as a means of becoming pure, but many people also demonstrate a fear of bacteria that borders on obsessive/ compulsive. People can't eat hamburgers by holding onto the bun but will only touch the wrapper. People won't grab a store door handle if at all possible but will instead try to slip in behind you. A woman I know scrubs suitcases after a trip, and I'm sure she is not alone. A casual stroll through the store will show you any number of products designed to kill germs, usually illustrated as tiny fanged demons.

You will also notice that cars are never dirty; many are proudly washed every week. A friend of mine spotted this conundrum on a junior high school English test: a picture of a polished car with the caption, "This car a) has been washed, or b) is going to be washed." As my friend pointed out, "In Japan, it could be either one."

CITY VS. COUNTRY

As one might expect in a country the size of California with a population of roughly 127 million, much of Japan is urban. Tokyo with its associated environs is the largest city in the world, and there are other cities of more than one million each. Consequently, most Japanese today have grown up being more familiar with a concrete pole than a rice stalk.

The traditional countryside (*inaka*), with its rice paddies and wooden houses framed by green mountains, is beautiful and tranquil. It is also anathema to what most Japanese consider to be the good life. Although most Tokyo residents have one complaint or another about

GIVE ME A SIGN: *No matter where you go in Japan, there's always a sign to show where you're going.*

the crush of city life, they certainly aren't in any hurry to get back to the countryside, either. There are many books that praise the Japanese traditional love of nature, but in actual practice there are a lot of people who feel uncomfortable in a natural setting. These people will avoid an extended time outdoors, finding it to be dirty, full of bugs, and without artificial lighting. City dwellers think country residents to be slow and their lives to be boring—why, you can't even begin to find name-brand goods in the hinterlands!

HUMAN NATURE

Bluntly speaking, the Japanese view of human nature is not a generous one to say the least. There is a tendency to think that, left to their own devices, people will sink to the basest level possible, or at least the dumbest one. Whether this is true is a matter for the philosophers; what is certain, however, is that it can be very insulting indeed.

In Japan, for example, road signs tell you what you *can* do, not what you can't. Blue signs at a certain intersection may indicate that you can go straight or turn left. How about a right turn? Well, if it's not indicated as being permissible, then forget about it—straight or left are the only available options.

And that, in a nutshell, is Japan: Everyone must always be checking to see what he is allowed to do. Even if he wasn't, someone would be telling him anyway. Signs in public parks will illustrate the correct way to swing one's arms while walking to get the maximum effect from the workout. Recorded voices over escalators will repeatedly drill home the message to be careful, perhaps on the off-chance that riders might suddenly forget how to get off. In fact, there is a recorded warning for just about *everything*. At a certain temperature my hot water heater will announce, "This temperature is hot. Do be careful." I'm sure there are some situations in which these announcements are valid; heck, maybe they all are. But their cumulative nattering leaves me wishing that all the machines would just break down and leave me in peace.

CHILDREN

While doing research I came across this sentence in another book: "Children are highly treasured in Japan." Gee, I wish my editor would let me get away with writing such a trite observation. As far as I can see, there are a lot of children who are highly treasured — just as they would be in any other part of the world. Unfortunately, there are also some who are just ignored, and sadly some who are treated quite badly indeed. You find good and bad parents everywhere in this life.

However, there are a few things particular to Japan that I've noticed in how parents raise their children:

- **A readiness to typecast.** Blue is for boys and pink is for girls, and don't ever think of raising your child otherwise. For my daughter's second birthday I gave her a baseball (there's never enough left-handed pitching in the majors) and the rest of the family was highly amused. Imagine teaching a girl how to throw a baseball!
- **An urge to micromanage.** A Canadian friend of mine was complimented on how her little girl showed such initiative in playing by herself in the park. My friend simply answered,

"That's because I let her." Too many mothers, it seems, hover over their little ones every step of the way and can't give their children a chance to grow up by themselves.

- **A tendency not to give children any responsibility.** There are a lot of children out there who are not required by their parents to do anything except study. Since, in Japan, the paths to success or failure are set rather early on in life, this perhaps makes much sense. However, it's really sad to see so many mothers who are at their child's beck and call. For some the dependency never ends; I know a 46-year-old woman who still has mommy make lunch for her everyday.

For children, the first few years are easy street. Then, as soon as they're ready for school, it's time to buckle down and study hard every day—so that when they're finished, they can get a job and work hard every day.

GETTING AHEAD. *Uniformed students follow the text while their teacher lectures.*

JAPANESE MEN

I teach English, and one lesson I had with a *sarariman* summed up, to me, the Japanese man's plight. I asked him very simply what time he got to work in the morning, and he answered, "Six o'clock."

Thinking he'd misheard the question, I said, "No, not what time you get up—what time do you get to work."

"Six o'clock."

It was I who had misunderstood. This man worked for a moving company in one of those hybrid white-collar/blue-collar positions, and every day he woke up at 5 a.m., got to work at six, worked until 11 p.m., and collapsed in bed at midnight. Six days. And as for Sunday? "I sleep all day." Of course he does.

Men in Japan, from the moment they get that full-time job, devote themselves to work. It may be because of tremendous peer and societal pressure, it may be because of internal expectations, but it happens regardless. Once in a while an English-language newspaper will run a story about how today's Japanese men are lightening up and taking things easier at work, which is kind of like writing a story about all the times that Donald Rumsfeld has shown flashes of cultural sensitivity. You may have seen it once, but it's going to be a long time before you can come up with another example.

Sure, men change jobs more than they used to, but lots of times that has simply been a matter of economic necessity: companies failed, bonuses just vanished, or even previously unheard-of layoffs took effect. In fact, the never-ending recession has enabled companies to —is this possible?—squeeze more productivity out of worried and nervous employees. There's no doubt about it; men work way past quitting time and rarely bother to claim all the overtime pay due them.

Or perhaps "work" is sometimes not the right word. I once worked as a consultant with a friend who worked at an advertising agency. His company was preparing an English-language publication for a certain company, and he asked me to vouch for the quality of the translation. During the three hours it took to satisfy the customer's every petty

PARTY BOYS. *At a "second party", a few drinks is all it takes for Japanese to overcome their legendary shyness.*

grammar question about a simple two-page publication, I was able to look around and see how hard the men in the office worked. The answer: not much. They sat around the office, occasionally checked their computers, and disappeared for interminable smoking breaks. I wanted to grab someone by the shoulders and shout, "Look — you're not doing much of anything. *Go home!*"

Obviously this is not representative of every office, because there are a lot of men who are overburdened to the point of exhaustion — and sometimes suicide. But a lot of companies have started to recognize that they're getting eight hours of work out of a 12-hour day, and they're trying to put a clamp on all of this. Some companies have begun a policy of locking the building and turning off the electricity by a certain hour to make sure their employees go home early at least once a week. And for many men who place too much of their identities in their companies, that's a hard thing to do.

One thing I have noted while living over here is the near-absence of a simple question we all heard as children: "What do you want to be when you grow up?" The answer might be fireman or doctor (in my case it was "paleontologist"), but the idea was to have the child identify what profession he'd like to take up in the future. In Japan, I was surprised how many office workers said they'd never heard that question once in their lives. There were expectations as to what university they'd attend, what company they'd like to work for, where they'd like to live—but the idea of identifying themselves with their chosen profession was unknown. What counted wasn't the job, it was the company.

And what is the result of all this devotion to duty? Well, so much time spent in one place can only mean time not spent in another. In this case it means the men simply aren't home most of the time, and when they are, they're too tired to do much. They are not greatly involved in household chores. A survey once asked men what household chores they performed, and the most common response was "put the *futon* away in the morning". At least they are doing something, I thought, until I realized that they couldn't put the *futon* away unless they were the last ones to wake up; their wives presumably were already making them breakfast. One popular slang word women have for men who lay around the house on Sunday is *sodai gomi*—"big garbage." They don't do anything except get in the way.

Nor do they even make much of an effort to help with their children. Fathers might be bawled out by their bosses for taking time off for "frivolous" pursuits such as attending a child's graduation. And though there are lots of caring fathers who use their precious free

ONE CHILD, TWO PARENTS. *Many couples today are choosing to have small families, if they have any children at all.*

time to do something with their families on Sundays, there's probably an equal number who deride this as "family service." For these men, it's like punching the clock.

Sometimes they learn too late. I was talking with one retired businessman about a famous *kabuki* drama, that of a samurai working for Lord A, but who must secretly save the life of Lord B's son. To satisfy Lord A's desire for revenge and simultaneously preserve Lord B's family line, he trickily substitutes the head of another little boy — that of his only son. Suddenly my student's eyes misted over. "I should have spent more time with my own family," he said.

I didn't know what to say.

JAPANESE WOMEN

There are two points of view regarding Japanese women. One camp holds that Japanese women are second-class citizens in their own country, invisibly bound by traditional dictates and consigned to a lifestyle of indulgent shopping and pretty irrelevance.

The other group also holds this to be true, but that they've still got things better than Japanese men do.

Only in Japan does it seem like the two sexes are instead two different species. For a start, women in Japan are expected to be extremely feminine. School uniforms for girls are skirts, never pants, and even a working woman in pants is a rare sight. Many walk in the traditional pigeon-toed, bow-legged manner called *uchimata*. In conversation with men, particularly customers, they are expected to speak with a high voice—some sound like they've just inhaled helium. If they laugh, many will hold their hands over their mouths. Most impressively, many women could not even begin to conceive of going out in public without makeup; I will often see a woman dressed to go hiking, or to work out, and be perfectly penciled and painted.

How one feels about the role and position of women in Japan depends in large part on one's own preconceptions. Is Japan a bastion of male-chauvinist pigs? Well, in company life, absolutely yes. Although laws were grudgingly passed outlawing sexual harassment in the work place, employment opportunities of prominence are terribly hard to come by. The postwar idea of the "office lady", or O.L. —someone who joins the company around the age of 20 and pours green tea for guests until marrying a company employee a few years later—remains strong to this day. Women are very visible in Japanese companies; it's just that their visibility is usually limited to roles where the company deems a softening femininity to be an asset: flight attendants, information desk clerks, elevator attendants, receptionists. Rarely are women allowed positions of authority, and even when they are, they are almost always put in charge of other women. It would seem that Japanese men have a pathological fear of having female bosses.

The single biggest structural weakness of Japanese society—an emasculated judiciary—shows itself when women are denied equal pay for equal work. Courts will reason, for example, that Man A was hired as a "management trainee" while Woman B was hired as a "desk operative", so even though they work side-by-side and do the same kind of work, their titles are different and therefore a difference in pay and benefits is allowed. To be a woman who wants to achieve great things in the world of Japanese business requires large amounts of talent, perseverance, connections, and luck. If she doesn't have all of those things, the system will find a way to grind her down.

But looked at another way, a lot of women see how dreadfully close to destruction many Japanese men are driven, and they quite sensibly opt out of that particular rat race. What woman could possibly balance the demands of a Japanese job AND devote suffi-cient care to her children AND handle the household tasks that her husband can't or won't do? The answer is "virtually no-one," of course. So a lot of women decide early on that the best choice is to find that up-and-coming executive, marry him, and then enjoy a life of shopping while the husbands toil. The dark underside to all this is that, if shrinking household purchasing power requires more women to work outside the home, if expensive brand-name goods are seen as a vital necessity, and if men refuse to assume more domestic chores, then many women avoid having children. Taking the husbands away from the home means dumping more responsibilities on the wives. This is one of the causes—perhaps the main cause—of Japan's perpetually shrinking pool of children, the 800-pound gorilla sitting on the back of Japan's future.

In corporate life, women are second-rate citizens, but as soon as one enters the front-door, it is the women who are in charge. Governments maintain power through control of the purse strings, and in Japan women really do control the "purse strings." Typically, men turn over their entire paychecks to their wives, and women in turn dole out an allowance to their husbands. This allowance may be pitifully small, and many husbands will have to go begging to their wives later, asking if they can get more money for nights out with the boys. (However, some men will let you know that they've managed over the years to build up a nest egg of their own, unbeknownst to their wives.)

Women can solely decide many facets of domestic life, from which apartment the family will purchase to which schools the children will attend. This tremendous power is of course balanced by a tremendous responsibility. If a child becomes sick, she may find herself blamed by her in-laws for not taking better care of her child's health. And if a child fails to enter a prestigious school, it is perceived as the mother's failure—she obviously did not instill enough self-discipline in her child to succeed.

So who has things better in Japan, men or women? I've met a few Western women who have seen how far men can go in society and have said they wished they had been born a man, but I don't think I've met the Japanese woman yet who has envied the life men endure. By contrast, I've met quite a few Japanese men who enviously see women shopping at fashionable department stores, dining at Italian restaurants, and going abroad with their friends. Societies everywhere have problems regarding gender roles; it is Japan's tragedy that people feel strongly trapped in theirs by others' expectations.

THE ELDERLY

Japan's population is the most rapidly aging in the world. This may not be readily apparent at first. Walking through the posh development Roppongi Hills, you might be forgiven if you thought everyone in the country was in his thirties. To find the elderly, you have to look in two places: the countryside and the hospitals.

The population's inexorable drift to the cities has left whole communities behind in the countryside that are dominated by the elderly. And, as retirement homes, old-age communities, and the like, are largely unknown, it has fallen to the hospitals to be the providers of last resort for Japan's elderly. Traditionally, it has been the responsibility of children (read: the eldest son's wife) to take care of

STORYTELLER. *Many older Japanese, like this man who briefly worked in California before the war, have fascinating tales to tell.*

aging parents. But social mores have changed; personally taking care of mother-in-law for 20 or 30 years is not what many wives look forward to doing. So the hospitals gladly provide peace of mind, knowing that under the present health system the government will just keep floating more bonds to pay for everything.

There are seemingly two sorts of Japanese people, post-retirement. One is the former company employee, who retired just before the age of 60. His wife raised two successful children; together, they led a life of conspicuous consumption. With a little money socked away, a company pension and government benefits, he is well positioned to play golf as much as he likes while his wife continues to pursue her hobbies and international vacations with her friends.

The other is the rural farmer or fisherman, who is just scraping by in an old house that's barely holding together. His children live far away, and he treads slowly through the town he's lived in all his life, totally unconnected to—and perhaps uncomprehending of—the changes that have convulsed Japan in the last 60 years.

To its credit, the government has recognized that this constant hollowing out of rural communities is leaving the elderly behind, and it has begun building facilities and training health care workers to take care of them. But there's an awful lot of catching up to be done.

GAYS AND LESBIANS

The idea of homosexuality or bisexuality can be initially shocking to many Japanese, as many of them have simply not even contemplated the concept. Historically, Japanese culture was not prejudiced against homosexuals, but starting around the Meiji period, that began to change, perhaps due to the importation of prevailing Western morality at that time.

Still, once people get over their initial shock there does seem to be less prejudice or resistance than in other countries. The idea seems to be, for example, that it's all right for a man to be gay, so long as he gets married and has children. You may think I'm joking but I'm not: One gay Western friend of mine had a Japanese boyfriend who was told to do exactly that. An elementary school teacher, he was being pressured by his parents and employer to get married, and he was making up his mind to enter an arranged marriage with the understanding that he would still be free to pursue his own life. My friend eventually persuaded him to give up that idea, but as you can see in Japan it's not so much one's personal beliefs that are problematic, it's just that people have to maintain proper form.

THE RIGHT WING

Japan has a noisy group of right-wingers. And I do mean noisy. Probably your only encounter with these extremists will be as they go driving their large sound trucks through the city. Painted in either white or black, with black curtains over the windows and decorated with slogans exalting the emperor and national values, they very s-l-o-w-l-y drive around with loudspeakers at full blast. They may be shouting some diatribe, or playing a patriotic song, but either way they seem intent on bullying the populace with sheer noise. I made the error once of obviously plugging my ears while waiting at a crosswalk for the truck to pass. The passenger grinned at me and impossibly turned the volume up.

It is important to note that, while various right-wing groups and gangster groups find it convenient to work with each other from time to time, they are not one and the same. Some time ago there was a fierce gun battle in Tokyo when some gangsters expected better terms for service than what they got, and pulled out their guns. Unfortunately for them they learned that the right-wingers had guns too, bigger and better machines than those carried by the gangsters.

YAKUZA

Japan's version of La Cosa Nostra is the *yakuza*. Like Mafiosi, they too are organized into crime families. While small in number, their influence is bigger than you might think.

Naturally, most of the obviously dodgy activities in society come under the purview of the *yakuza*, such as drug dealing, prostitution,

SERVICE CALLS. *Stickers mysteriously appear inside pay phone booths in the early evening, advertising "companionship".*

pornography, gambling, extortion, and loan sharking. They are also big-time operators in the construction industry. Worse, it seems that many *yakuza* groups, flush with cash collected over the years, have investments in so many legitimate concerns in Japan and abroad that it is difficult to extricate their tentacles from legitimate businesses.

This is Japan; even gangsters have to look the part. The typical older *yakuza* wears an expensive dark suit and sunglasses and keeps his hair in a tight permanent wave. He will have a tattoo—sometimes a whole set decorating his back—and as he walks through Japan the crowds will part before him. No one, it seems, wants to confront one of these guys.

A lesser form of the *yakuza* is known as *chimpira*. Kind of like *yakuza* wanna-bes, these younger guys are found at the lower rungs of criminal activity. Their most visible activity is loitering around train stations in sharp clothes, looking to recruit young women for employment as bar hostesses or worse.

GANGS

Japan does have its youth gangs, although their activities are nowhere near as dangerous as those of, say, Los Angeles. Known as *bousouzoku*, their most visible activity is racing their motorbikes or cars through the cities at night, often to the cheers of their friends and girlfriends. The racing makes for a common urban disturbance, and there are frequent complaints from other residents that the police are just flat-out ineffectual in dealing with the problem. Unable to catch the bikers themselves, the police worked instead to pass a law making it illegal for pedestrians to cheer bikers.

There have been more serious incidents in which gang members have attacked homeless people, foreigners, and ordinary business-men. Although the problem overall is very small, pay attention to your surroundings, particularly after midnight.

DIRTY OLD—AND NOT SO OLD—MEN

Roughly translated as "perverts", *chikan* are the men who grope women on morning trains or evening walks, flash their private parts in a park, or perform some other lewd act in public. Most foreign women will not have to cope with this—certainly not to the extent that Japanese women have to—but be aware of it just the same. Packed trains make it especially difficult to identify an offender; one woman I know felt the best way to cope with the problem was to grab the man's hand and bite it. Hard.

Not to be confused with *chikan* are *sukebe*, guys who either have a raunchy mouth or manner, but who carry on with such a humorous air that they're considered all right party people, just one of the boys.

FOREIGNERS

"Who are you?" asked one British band famously, and at some point in Japan you might be asking yourself the same question. (If you start answering, however, I can't help you anymore.) Probably one of the first Japanese words you will learn is *gaijin*. *Gaijin* literally means "outside person", and it denotes everyone who isn't Japanese. Of course it can also mean the second-, third-, and even fourth-generation Koreans and Chinese who have lived in Japan all their lives and are about as "inside" as one can get, but never mind. *Gaijin*, however, is usually tossed at the foreigner who looks physically different from the Japanese. Over my years in Japan I have come to hear this much less in public, even from the schoolchildren who used to shriek, "*Gaijin da!*" ("It's a foreigner!") I would often feign shock and exclaim, "*Nihonjin da!*" ("It's a Japanese!")

Foreigners who stay in Japan for any length of time will undoubtedly experience the wild yo-yo of being alternately admired and scorned, liked and disliked. For one thing, I've never seen an Asian country in which foreign models, particularly ones with blond hair and blue eyes, are so conspicuous in both print and television advertising. Yet the same person might find himself sitting on a train

YES, I CAN USE CHOPSTICKS. *Many Japanese are surprised that Westerners can eat with chopsticks.*

and suddenly wonder why all the seats have been taken—except for the ones right around him. If he's of African extraction, he may find that he is the epitome of cool for the younger generation—but let him go into a shop and he may be carefully watched for shoplifting.

Foreigners are envied because of their ability to ignore the conventions of Japanese culture. They are also pitied ... because of their inability to understand the conventions of Japanese culture. Speak a few words of Japanese and you will be applauded; learn the language fluently and you will undoubtedly fluster someone who realizes you're starting to catch on to what people are actually saying and doing.

There are foreigners in Japan who will stuffily insist that the correct term for foreigners is *gaikokujin*, or "outside-country person". Anything else, and they wind up in a snit. My feeling about this battle over terminology is that these people are the same sort of hypersensitive people who need to take a Valium or three. Any word can be used lovingly or hatefully; it all depends on the speaker's intent. Most Japanese do not mean to give offense when they say "gaijin", and if they do it's blatantly obvious. Otherwise, don't let it worry you, and if you can't do that just remember how the main character in Owen

Wister's classic cowboy novel, *The Virginian*, dealt with someone who called him a dirty name. He looked the offender in the eye for a good while and calmly said, "When you call me that, smile!"

What Japanese Think of Non-Japanese

This topic title may strike some of you as being a little bit unfair—that one could even begin to generalize about the feelings of 120 million people. However, it's not me who has first labeled the Japanese as thinking alike—it's the Japanese themselves. If I had a grain of rice for every time I heard Japanese people begin a sentence by saying "We Japanese ...", I could open a sushi shop. Japanese people are so conditioned into thinking they all think alike that it almost feels unfair not to take them at their word.

Let's see ... where did my original topic go? Oh, yes ... it seems there are only two prevailing views of foreigners. One group holds that foreigners are friendlier and more open with their emotions. They are fun and lead lives of excitement. They are not secretive. They say what they are thinking. They are kind to strangers. They don't feel bound to do what everyone else does.

The other group thinks foreigners complain too much. Or that they are lazy and always finding a way not to work. Or that they are extremely cheap and will niggle over the smallest expense. Or that they can only find fault with Japan, not their own countries. Or that they are full of pride. Or that they are simply untrustworthy. I was once supposed to meet a couple of students for dinner but had to cancel at the last moment because of work. One student's mother told her, "I told you so. You can never trust a *gaijin*." Of course Japanese men miss appointments all the time because of last-minute job obligations, but then that's the double standard at work.

Looking at yourself through the lens of another culture is an educative process for many people who come to Japan. How you go about answering people's misconceptions about you may go a long way to helping you understand who you really are.

CONVERSATIONAL TOPICS

Initial topics of conversation with people are startlingly identical no matter where you go or whom you meet. Inevitably, the first question is, "Where are you from?" (which, it must be said, is a vast improvement from many years ago: "Are you American?") Other common questions will be about your age, height, job, marital status, children, hobbies, and whether you like Japanese food or can use chopsticks. If the same questions recur time and again, it is because people are generally curious, or they're trying to figure out where you fit into in society, or they're doing their best to be polite by expressing an interest in you, genuine or not.

Japanese people generally avoid political or religious topics in conversation. They may express approval or disapproval of a particular prime minister, and they may blandly identify their own religion, but they seem definitely aware that such topics can be polarizing when explored in detail, and that it's best to discuss them only between very close friends.

Controversial Topics

There are quite a few topics with which foreigners can upset Japanese complacency. Tops on the list would be Japan's treatment of its Korean population. Koreans comprise the largest number of non-Japanese in Japan. What makes this unusual, however, is that these holders of Korean passports have lived in Japan for two, three, or four generations. Many of their ancestors were brought to Japan as slave labor, and after the war their descendants stayed. Today, their children will grow up in Japan, speak Japanese, and be virtually indistinguishable from their Japanese friends—but even to this day they are not fully accepted by the rest of Japanese society.

Japan does have its outcasts, called *burakumin*. These are the descendants of people who generations ago performed "unclean" tasks, according to Buddhist practices, such as slaughtering animals or leatherwork. Today, this distinction has ABSOLUTELY NO

MEANING WHATSOEVER—and yet top employers will quietly deny them good jobs, and parents of prospective suitors will nix a wedding if their prospective in-laws are of this group. Some Japanese really don't know anything about this topic; some just say that they don't.

Other uncomfortable topics might include teenaged prostitution, sex trafficking, corruption, pervasive criminality, and industrial pollution. Oh, yes, and the war.

As an American, I had vague misgivings that somehow I would be heckled in Hiroshima and Nagasaki by angry protesters upset about the conclusion of World War II. Nothing could be further from the truth. I do find a little resentment when I visit Hiroshima, but that seems to be more a product of the U.S. military presence based nearby than from any historical animosity. But otherwise the war is a subject that, while not a topic that you'd pull out on a first meeting, can be discussed with sensitivity and without recrimination.

My boss in Nagasaki was an elderly man who, on the very first day we met, explained how he was a boy in the mountains on 9 August 1945 and saw the atomic bomb detonated. "My house was destroyed. Many of my friends died," he said with a trace of sadness that seemed to never have left him. I didn't know what to say, although deep inside me I wanted to shout, "I didn't do it!" Then I realized that, except for the disappearing survivors, most people today have no direct experience with that time, either. We are all merely participants in the war's legacy.

What was described at the time as the "fanaticism" of the typical Japanese soldier during the war seems in retrospect to be simple heroism. If Japan's soldiers did not play by expected "rules of war", it must also be added that they did not expect to be given any quarter either. And as for the vicious and sadistic treatment meted out to Allied POWs, it must be noted that Japan's military was not always regarded as savage; the Russian captives of 1905 found themselves well-treated at the hands of Japanese soldiers under the command of legendary gentleman General Nogi. That Japanese soldiers committed atrocious, barbaric acts during World War II is true, but much of that blame must be placed squarely upon the shoulders of the officers who oversaw a brutal military training system.

Keep in mind that while most Japanese have some idea that their armies did terrible things abroad, few people today really *know*. One of my good friends, a very educated young teacher, returned from her trip to Singapore in tears. She'd visited its notorious wartime prison museum. "I didn't have any idea," she lamented. If you think people lack your all-balanced point of view, give them the benefit of the doubt and blame it on an education policy that tightly controls what people should be taught.

BOWING

Unless you meet a Japanese who insists on being hip and extending his arm for a handshake, you will have to greet and leave people by bowing. The bow is not terribly difficult, although it may take a little practice to get the hang of it. For either gender, it is entirely correct to keep the arms at the sides while bending from the waist to a 45-degree angle. Women only may execute a more formal bow by holding one hand with the other, palms inward, just below the waist and bowing to the same angle, elbows compressing ever so slightly.

There are two rules that are important when bowing:

1) Resist the temptation to lift your eyes and keep them focused straight ahead. Instead, let your eyes naturally point downward as you bow.

2) A subordinate should bow at least marginally lower than a superior. Take a quick peek to make sure that you adjust accordingly.

If all this sounds like a Catch-22 and that you can't do No.2 while performing No. 1, well, that's Japan. You're going to have to work it out yourself.

In daily life, people are forever bowing, though the bows may be less formally executed than as explained above. A person saying goodbye to another on the street may depart with a series of "half-bows" while excusing himself. A driver may pause at a crosswalk and bow to let a pedestrian cross, while the pedestrian will hurry across and simultaneously attempt a bow in return. Even more charmingly, people bow on the telephone as they say their goodbyes and hang up!

A complement to all of this is that, when formally leaving a room, one shouldn't depart with one's back to the group but rather exit by opening the door, turning to face the group, and then bowing and stepping backward through the door.

MANNERS

Culturally, of course, Japan is famed for its high degree of etiquette and manners. However, what a Westerner might consider good and bad manners, and what a Japanese person might regard as such, can sometimes be very much at odds with each other.

For one thing, blowing one's nose in public, particularly at the dining table, is considered extremely rude. Personally, I try to maintain a balance between what I consider good manners and what are considered good manners in Japan, and this is one rule that I steadfastly adhere to: If I have to blow, to the restroom I go.

Yet it is seemingly acceptable for people to sniffle constantly. Rather than take care of their noses by blowing once and being done with it, they'd rather aggravate everyone else in the room with their sniffing. My mother wouldn't last a day over here during flu season before she'd accost some startled person and say, "I can't stand that noise anymore—go blow your nose!"

Walking down the street can pose another problem. Because Japan places a premium on the egalitarianism of the group, you will as often as not see a group of five *sararimen* walking toward you five abreast—not one of them ahead or behind the other. This might not be a problem were they walking down the Champs Elysées, but on the narrow sidewalks of Japan they look like an American football team ready to sack you, the opposing quarterback. The first time I saw this, I remembered that in *Star Wars*, sandpeople ride their banthas single-file to hide their numbers, and thought that perhaps this was the whole point—in Japan, the group *wants* to announce its numbers. Unperturbed, I charged straight for the middle of the pack and broke the line.

In general, men can get away with a lot more disgusting behavior in public than women can. Men don't try to spit in the gutter or the drain; anywhere on the sidewalk will do. At night, men can piss on the sides of buildings if they can't be bothered to find a restroom, and they can puke their guts out on train platforms or even the trains themselves if they've drunk too much. And I've had to sit next to too many men on the train who found it imperative to thoroughly clean their nose with their fingers.

Be aware that eating and walking at the same time in public is thought to be bad manners, although this rule may be starting to break. And, as in the rest of Asia, using one's feet to accomplish any sort of task, whether it be pointing or changing channels on the TV remote control, is considered extremely rude.

Smoking

One of the very few things that will likely be less expensive in Japan than in your home country is tobacco. Cigarettes are cheap, even with the marginal increase in the tobacco tax, and are widely available, thanks to the proliferation of cigarette vending machines. Although the machines are slated for eventual removal, like anything else in Japan, it will take time.

Smoking is widespread in Japan, much more than in Europe and far more than in the U.S. If you're a smoker, you're in luck; if you're not, you may find yourself in situations where the only thing that can spare you secondhand smoke is the courtesy of the smoker.

Smoking is not permitted at all on Japan's domestic or international flights, with the rare exception of some small local routes. Smoking is generally not allowed on private rail lines, and is permitted on JR trains only in specially designated cars. On train platforms and in airports, smoking is allowed only in "smokers' corners." Additionally, many municipalities recently have passed laws that forbid smoking, or smoking while walking, within certain city areas. Fines are usually mild, but may be assessed should a police officer spot you smoking in one of them.

And that is about the limit of the restrictions. Most restaurants have no rules whatsoever regarding smoking, and only family restaurants consistently make an effort to designate smoking and nonsmoking areas. Despite that, you may find that your "nonsmoking table" is immediately next to the smoking section, and even if it is not you may find that you have to wade through the smoking section in order to reach your table. Bars of course do not restrict smoking, and coffee shops are a notorious den for smokers (Starbuck's being a notable exception).

Even hospitals allow smoking within certain zones. Perhaps it is because so many doctors themselves are heavy smokers, or perhaps it is simply a concession to the fact that a lot of patients are set in their ways and aren't going to change, but regardless, widespread smoking is one of the darker blots on Japan's international image. One reason for that is that Japan Tobacco is actually a government-owned monopoly which reaps enormous profits from tobacco sales. The country's incidence of lung cancer is ascending, and what is worse is that many young women are joining the heretofore predominantly male ranks of smokers. Ten years ago you wouldn't see young women walk down the street with a cigarette in their hands. Now you do.

If you're in a place where smoking is not permitted, you can remind a smoker about the pertinent rules by pointing to the no-smoking sign. And if you're in an area where there are no rules, but you'd still like your neighbor to refrain from smoking, you can politely ask him to stop. Many Japanese are aware that a lot of foreigners are not appreciative of secondhand smoke and will cease if asked.

JAPANESE AND THE LAW

Let me tell you a wonderful little story: During my first week in Japan, I absent-mindedly lost my camera bag, complete with my beloved SLR camera with its wide-angle and telephoto lenses, at a tourist attraction. I didn't even notice until one day later, and when I did my sudden realization was instantly followed by the shattering regret that it was likely gone and gone for good.

The next day it was delivered to my hotel. With more foresight than I am usually capable of mustering, I had tucked a hotel matchbook into the camera bag pocket on the chance that I got lost and needed someone to point me in the right direction. The person who found my camera bag obviously found the matchbook, noted the address, and returned the bag with everything inside it. I still don't know whom to thank.

That's the story that I have kept in mind, even after having my scooter helmet lifted, an umbrella or two nicked, my wallet swiped, and my scooter stolen. In every case it was a matter of me leaving something of worth available for easy, unobtrusive pickings. In Japan, like every other country, people steal what is necessary or valuable. My camera may have been returned because of the fundamental honesty of the person. Or, it might have been returned because, in a country where everyone has a camera and a used product two years old has little intrinsic value, it wasn't wanted anyway.

Years ago, one of the images of the lawful Japanese seared into my brain was of a man waiting patiently at a crosswalk for the light to change, even though there was not a car in sight. I still see this from time to time, but mostly that image has gone glimmering. Now I see people who, American-style, ascertain that no cars are coming before confidently walking against a red light. People smoke in no-smoking zones, fish from right next to no-fishing signs, and park their cars and bikes directly underneath signs that proclaim no parking.

What's going on? Are the Japanese really an anarchic people? Well, to a greater extent than you might have thought possible, yes.

Rustheap. *Despite the environmental P.R., many Japanese avoid recycling fees by dumping their old cars in remote areas.*

Put it this way: If there is a situation in which another's rights would be directly and adversely affected, then Japanese people respect those rights. For example, Japanese would almost never park their cars on a private parking lot full of empty parking spaces, because to do so would obviously infringe on someone's private property. Were they to be called to account, they would certainly lose face and have to embarrassedly retreat.

But infringing on public rights is an entirely different matter, perhaps because, as some have suggested, Japanese society really has trouble identifying a "public" realm that is completely separate from all of society's competing "private" realms. The fisherman who fishes out of the public pond despite the signs forbidding him to do so — who's going to call him to account? Whom is he directly hurting? Apart from the fish, that is.

Chapter Three

SOCIALIZING WITH
THE JAPANESE

DURING THE MEAL GO AROUND THE TABLE ON YOUR KNEES WITH THE BEER...

NOT 'AFTER' LIKE AT HOME.

TRIGG

"In matters of grave importance, style, not sincerity, is the vital thing."

–Oscar Wilde

ENTERTAINING AT HOME

The first rule about entertaining at home is quite simple: Most people don't do it. The obvious reason is that living accommodations are cramped enough without having to worry about bringing guests in. The other reason, however, is that an invitation into another person's home is an eventful step. Crossing that Rubicon—or at least that doorway—shows a change in the relationship.

If you do entertain at home, be aware that you cannot simply place an unopened drink or a snack in front of someone and say, "Help yourself." People need to be bidden to do so simply because it's good manners for them to refuse at least once, so you must ask them to do so up to three times. (If, after three times, they still refuse, that is definitely a sign that they don't want it!)

Another thing that doesn't really work is the Western idea of a snack or hors d'oeuvres before a meal, particularly before all of the other guests have arrived. It is deeply ingrained that everyone at a party should all sit down and eat together, so very likely the most you will be able to get your first-arriving guest to take before dinner is a drink.

I would especially recommend trying to figure out what your guests like to eat. Just as there are Westerners who can't bring themselves to try Japanese food, there are also Japanese who don't really like foreign food. Some will even eat before visiting another person's home, in the fear that they won't like their host's food.

For many Japanese, no meal is satisfying unless it's accompanied by a bowl of rice. I found this out the hard way when, as a thank-you to the people who had helped me move, I arranged a Western-style picnic Sunday afternoon luncheon at my house: cold cuts and cheeses, different kinds of bread, potato salad, and other vegetables. My guests sat around and politely munched at the food, and then one of them asked to use my phone. About 20 minutes later a large delivery order from the nearby Japanese restaurant arrived, and my guests happily consumed it. To say I was dumbfounded is an understatement.

ENTERTAINING OUT

Most social events for Japanese people will take place in restaurants, in hotel banquet rooms, or at public facilities. Be on time—Japan is not the place where people make fashionably late appearances. People will first greet each other by bowing, and then there will be the inevitable milling around until it is time for the party to begin.

If it is a traditional Japanese party known as an *enkai*, you will find yourself kneeling or sitting cross-legged in front of a small table.

SNACKING. *The "snack" is a small bar wih small sofas and small plates of junk food. The only thing that isn't small is the bill.*

Before eating or drinking, however, someone will make a speech welcoming everyone to the party. Pray that it is a short one, and not one of the leg-numbingly long speeches that too many people are prone to making. There is also the possibility that each party member will give a short self-introduction. Unless you've been told otherwise, you needn't say much more than your name, your company or school, if you are a student, where you are from, and thanks for being invited.

Do not partake of food or drink until commanded by your host to do so. Even then it is polite to hold back until others have started. It is not a bad idea to avoid eating slowly; if it's a procession of courses they will be whisked in and out, and in any case there is always a strict deadline for getting a party done and over with.

The drinking routine is, uh, routine. Large brown bottles of beer will be placed before you. Do NOT attempt to open one and start guzzling it by yourself! Instead, open the bottle and pour the beer into the glasses of the people seated around you—the more beer you pour, the more Brownie points you can earn. After the speech, you should raise your glass in a toast and say cheers ("*Kampai!*"), touching glasses with your neighbors and swallowing as much as you can. If you're a non-drinker, it is expected that you at least raise your beer glass to your lips. After that, you are entirely allowed to look for another glass and fill it with orange soft drink or oolong tea (there will always be some available). Otherwise, feel free to go ahead alternately drinking and pouring beer with your neighbors.

At some point you should grab a full bottle of beer and make your way around the table (if it's a low table, doing so on your knees) to top off the glasses of good friends and senior members of your organization. Happily flattered at your demonstrable mastery of the intricacies of Japanese culture, they in turn will grab an extra glass and pour for you, expecting you to join them for a mini toast and a short conversation. Drink as much or as little as you like; you're going to need the stamina later on.

During the party, *sake* and *shouchuu* will also make their appearance. While I found a bit of *sake* to be no problem, most people in Japan seem unaware of the problems resulting from too many alcohols mixed together. If you insist on sticking to only one type of alcoholic drink, you will seem a bit odd, but that's all.

A second party almost always follows the first one. Yet you may notice that the number of people who arrive for the second party (*nijikai*) is much smaller than the number of people who left the first one, ostensibly headed for the *nijikai*. What happens is that those people can't directly say that they're dissing the *nijikai*. Instead they walk at the end of the train of people heading for the second party, dropping further and further behind, until they can discreetly slip down an alley and escape any further obligation. Equally politely, the people who do make it to the *nijikai* never take notice of their absence. For the easily noticed foreigner, though, it's a bit harder—though not impossible—to pull the same stunt.

GIFT DOS AND DON'TS

Gifts are tremendously important in Japan; why, without them, perhaps half the country's elected leaders would be motivated to find other employment.

Whoops! Pardon me! Seriously, though, gift-giving in Japan is just a manifestation of the giver's well-wishes toward the recipient, just as it would be in any other part of the world. That gifts in Japan tend to be more expensive, that they are expected in more situations than you might otherwise expect ... well, that's just Japan.

Unlike, for example, the U.S., where a new resident might be greeted by his neighbors bearing cakes or pies, in Japan it is the newcomer who is expected to present gifts to the "group" he or she is joining. That means visiting, at a minimum, the neighbors on each side of your apartment or house and presenting a small gift. It really doesn't have to be much; in fact, you'd be surprised how often people in various gift-giving situations get away with giving a small white towel.

It is also a good idea, if you are to begin working in Japan, to present a gift to the person or people who will have direct responsibility for you. In practical terms that means, if your boss is the typical middle-aged manager, a gift of foreign whiskey or cigarettes — the more exclusive, the better.

The presentation of the gift is even more important than the gift itself. Whatever you do, do NOT present your gift to one person in front of everyone else, and loudly proclaim what an expensive present it is that you labored mightily to find. You will quickly, if unknowingly, earn the wrath of jealous co-workers and embarrass your recipient no end. Instead, find a moment when you can approach the person one-on-one and quietly present it. Be also sure to politely denigrate your gift as is customary; it gives the recipient the opportunity to protest that he's not worthy of your gift, and both parties can feel flattered by the other's kindness. If you're giving someone the

Hope Diamond, just announce it as a trifle you found lying on the ground; if someone presents you with cat hairballs, say how they are the finest hairballs you've ever received.

Wrapping is also essential to the gift-giving procedure. Most every shop will wrap a gift if asked, and unlike Western department stores with their separate gift-wrapping counters, it can usually be handled at any counter. (But please not when I'm the customer immediately following you!) Some shops don't wrap *per se* but simply put the item in one of the store's more fashionable bags; this is considered very acceptable.

For employees, there are two particular seasons in which they are expected to present their employers with gifts. Called *o-chuugen* and *o-seibo*, they are times when the good worker should give his boss a present to thank him for his support. Good ideas for presents include boxes of several different kinds of food, coffee, or beer; you can find display packages in the window of every department store during

NOT ANOTHER GIFT-GIVING SEASON! *Department stores display suitable gifts for semiannual presents to one's boss.*

each gift-giving season. The period for *o-chuugen* lasts from 1 July to 15 August; *o-seibo* from 1 December until the last day the company is open for the year. Coincidentally or not, that is also the time of year that employees receive their semi-annual bonuses.

Employees are also expected, if they go traveling for business or pleasure, to return with presents for everyone in the office. These souvenirs, called *o-miyage*, are usually in the form of boxes containing numerous individually wrapped crackers, cookies, or cakes. Every port, station, airport, resort, and tourist trap will have its inevitable collection of locally-produced souvenirs. Some of them can be tasty, but others seem merely an excuse to perpetuate bad food. Whatever you buy, make sure you buy enough to give one to each person you work with; trust me, there's always one more person to give a present to than you can remember while you're traveling.

One gift to avoid is any kind of plant with roots to a person ill in the hospital; the roots symbolize that the illness has taken root in the person and is not going away. Cut flowers, however, are acceptable. And never, ever give presents in sets of four or nine, as those numbers are considered unlucky. You'll notice after a while that things which you might expect to be sold in sets of four or six as they are in the West are instead sold in groups of five in Japan. Odd numbers are favored over even numbers by the Japanese.

Valentine's Day can present a tricky situation for women, as they are expected to give chocolate to men. For friends, lovers, and spouses this is no problem, but women are also expected to give presents to their male colleagues and bosses, even if they think some of them are the most disgusting creeps they've ever met. In Japan there is even a word for this kind of present: *giri-choco*, the obligatory chocolate that is given just to go through the motions of giving. The one saving grace out of all this is that the men are expected to reciprocate on White Day (14 March) with presents of cookies or cakes for the ladies.

The other important gift-giving season is New Year's, when children through high school age are given small envelopes stuffed

WHERE BETTER THAN A TENNIS BAR
TO FIND 'LOVE'?

with cash called *o-toshidama*. The amount you give depends on your closeness to the child, but it would be very unlikely that you would be expected to give more than a couple of thousand of yen to each child.

SOCIALIZING, JAPANESE STYLE

As one might expect, socializing between the sexes can be a problem in such a ritualistic, formal culture as Japan's. It's not that the barriers between people are insurmountably high; it's just that people believe they are. (How else can one explain the practicality of paper doors?) Accordingly, people will resist even the simplest ways of reaching out to each other because they haven't yet been properly introduced.

Young Japanese who wish to meet eligible partners often do so in the comfort of a *gou-kon*. This is like a double or triple date with no preconception as to who might be interested in whom. Sometimes they work, sometimes they don't. More elaborate are the *gou-kon* parties which bring together larger numbers of men and women hoping to find a suitable partner for marriage. There may be no one who finds the right mate, but there will certainly be someone who made a profit on the party.

Popular ways of getting together for singles include karaoke, hikes, tennis, and parties at restaurants or pubs.

WEDDINGS

It is entirely possible to get married in Japan with a minimum of fuss. All that is required is for the couple to fill out the relevant document from the local city or town office, and then get the signatures of two witnesses. Bingo! You're done. (And, it should be added, a divorce of a Japanese marriage in which no children or property are contested can also be accomplished in the same minimal manner.)

However, you might not have guessed that fact, certainly not after staring at the countless adverts for weddings in magazines and inside commuter train cars. Weddings are very big business in Japan, and it would seem that the media does conspire to convince a Japanese woman that the be-all and end-all of her life is to have a spectacular, Hollywood-style wedding production that will leave her guests with mouths agape. (The drudgery that is expected of every young housewife the day after her day of bliss is somehow glossed over.)

The actual wedding itself will usually involve only family and close friends, and it will take place at one of two places: either at the traditional location of a Shintou shrine, or at the increasingly fashionable "Christian" chapels that many hotels maintain as part of their wedding package service. Why so many Japanese couples would opt for a Christian-style wedding—when only about one percent of the Japanese population is Christian—is puzzling, but it is obvious that the trappings of a Christian service satisfy a particular need.

After the wedding comes the inevitable wedding party. Most couples will arrange for a party to be held at a large hall in a major hotel; a few opt for a reservation at a fine restaurant. Hotel weddings will have more opportunities for glitz and glamour than restaurant parties, but in either place you will likely be impressed by the dinner, the emcee's running commentary, and the slide show detailing how the bride and groom grew up to reach this point. Note that the bride will usually enter the hall in traditional kimono, step out to return dressed in a white wedding dress, and then step out again to return one last time in an evening gown. Like I said, it's a production!

MARRIAGE, JAPANESE STYLE. *Bride and groom, flanked by their attendants, stand before the assembled guests at the reception.*

When not entering or departing or performing some other action, the bride and groom will be seated at the front table, together with the man and woman known as *nakoudo*. These people have something akin to the function of the best man and maid of honor in a Western wedding; however, they are usually not friends of the couple but instead elder friends of the family who can lend an air of respectability to the proceedings. Close relatives will be seated at the tables farthest away from the couple so that honored guests, such as office superiors or business associates, might have the best seats.

During lulls in the action, it is permissible, even encouraged, for the guests to approach the table where the bride and groom are seated and offer to pour them a fresh glass of beer or wine. However, it would probably be best to keep your congratulations short and to the point —both of them, and especially the bride, may be so busy thanking everyone that they don't even time to eat their own dinners. I came that close to missing out on eating our own wedding cake.

In Japan, the only gifts that are typically given at weddings are gifts of money—no need to go shopping beforehand for a toaster or the like. A cash gift might seem rather cold, but what the guests are in effect doing is paying for their dinners. The couple will throw a good party for their guests (one hopes!), and all the guests can do is make sure that the couple doesn't begin life together already deeply in debt. The absolute minimum gift one should consider making is 10,000 yen, and 20,000 yen would be far preferable, since that is about the minimum per person charge that a couple can negotiate with the hotel. A rough guide that Japanese people themselves will use is that people in theirs 20s should give 20,000, thirtysomethings should give 30,000, and so on.

Your gift (in denominations of 10,000 yen) should be placed in a traditional red and white envelope, which you can find at any stationery shop or convenience store. Carefully place the enclosed band over the envelope and present the gift at the table just outside the

ANYONE FOR SECONDS? *A multiplicity of dishes awaits the invitee at a wedding banquet. Bring your appetite.*

hall where friends of the bride and groom are helping out. After that, just enjoy the party, and when departing make sure you bow to give your thanks and congratulations to the young couple and their parents.

Some people who have been to many wedding parties complain that there is too little variety between them; once you've seen one, you've seen them all. It is true that couples who put very little effort between them into their weddings wind up with cookie-cutter parties, but it is also true that couples who personalize their weddings can count on the hotel's staff to professionally create a memorable event for everyone. Another good point about weddings in Japan occurs during the middle of the party, when guests are invited to "sing for their supper", as it were. One of the most enjoyable days I've ever had in Japan was attending a colleague's wedding with two British friends and standing up in front of everyone to sing the three vocal parts of "Blue Moon" together. No, we didn't win a recording contract after the performance, but that's not the point. In Japan, you should never feel too embarrassed to try something fun, because people will always support you if you're willing to give it a go.

After the wedding party comes the second party, either directly following or at some later point during the day. It will usually be held at some classy bar or pub. The second party offers the bride and groom a chance to relax and interact with their guests in a way that they couldn't during the first party. Additionally, the second party allows the groom's female friends, and the bride's male friends, a chance to congratulate the couple; traditionally, it is frowned upon for those friends to be invited to the wedding party itself. The second party may devolve into a third party if enough people agree to it, but at some point the young couple will slip away and let their friends carry on without them.

How do people get around to getting married? Well, in addition to what are called "love marriages" (i.e., the husband and wife met on their own and fell in love), there are also arranged marriages. Called *o-miai*, arranged marriages are meetings set up between two people who want to get married but don't know how to go about meeting an eligible partner. These meetings can be set up by the prospective partners' parents, or even a professional network. Usually there will be one, two, or at most three meetings, after which it's time for each person to decide if they could live with the other for life. If not, it's time to say goodbye and move on to the next arranged meeting.

Many arranged marriages are the result of parental pressure. One friend of mine was told by her mother that, if she could get married within the coming year, she would give her a sizable amount of money. My friend didn't take her mother up on her offer, but her single status additionally caused trouble for her younger sister. The sister wanted to get married, but as her older sister was still single, the younger woman had to ask permission of her older sister before she could get married. To act precipitously and neglect to ask, she worried, would cause her older sister tremendous grief. That terrific mental dance that Japanese people work themselves into before ever uttering a word was on display in this situation, and quite needlessly as usual. As my friend commented, "I really didn't care if she got married first."

FUNERALS

Getting married is one of life's options; dying isn't. At some point you may be compelled to attend someone's wake or funeral while in Japan.

Death is disposed of in lightning time, at least as far as Westerners are concerned. My colleague died on Monday afternoon. His wake was Tuesday evening and his funeral was Wednesday morning. Everything was completed within 48 hours.

Most wakes and funerals are Buddhist, and even some families that are nominally Christian or Shintoist will wind up having a Buddhist presence somewhere. They will likely be held at a funeral hall. You should present a small present in a special envelope, similar to the one used for weddings, except that this one will be bordered with black and silver. The present is a gift of cash: 5,000 yen for a family member or close colleague, 3,000 yen for someone of passing acquaintance. Do NOT give 4,000 yen, as the number four has especially unlucky connotations. In return, you will likely be invited to eat and drink with the family and other guests. It would be impolite to refuse; it would also be impolite to attack the meal as an all-you-can-eat buffet.

At some ceremonies you will approach an altar to make a prayer. Sometimes there is incense powder to spread on the burner, sometimes a joss stick to be lit and then extinguished with your left hand. Observe what the other people do and follow accordingly. You will also have an opportunity to talk with the deceased's family. There are stock expressions for moments like these, but a short moment to express your personal memories and regard for the deceased is of course highly appreciated.

GRAVE MOMENTS. *Family graves are constantly cleaned and decorated with flowers.*

Since cremation in Japan is done at a comparatively low temperature, the bones of the deceased will not be completely consumed. Instead, it is the duty of the immediate family members to break those bones apart by hand into smaller pieces. As shocking as that might seem, if you are so asked to join you should find the strength to honor the dead as the others do.

As you leave, or perhaps when you check your mail later, you will receive a small gift—some tea, perhaps, plus a small package of salt. The salt is used to throw over your shoulder and ward off any spirit of death that might be following you home from the funeral. Do not, however, write a note to the family thanking them for the gift.

In addition, Buddhist tradition demands periodic anniversary events to mark someone's death. These will occur on the first, third, fifth, seventh, and thirteenth anniversaries and sometimes beyond. So don't be puzzled when your friend turns down your invitation with the explanation, "I can't meet you on Saturday. My grandfather died last year."

Chapter Four

ACCOMMODATION

TRIGG.

" … what Westerners would regard as little more than
rabbit hutches."
    –EC Commission report about Japanese housing

Famously labeled "rabbit hutches", Japanese housing can nevertheless be satisfying, should you have the urge to live like a *bonsai* tree.
You may visit an apartment billed as having a combined living room,
dining room and kitchen. As you inspect the place, you may think,
"Well, here's the kitchen—where are the living room and dining
room?" Then the realization dawns that you're looking at all three at
once. And it may be advertised as having three bedrooms, but at first
sight you think the bedrooms are closets.

   Not only is horizontal space usually lacking, but it can be missing
vertically as well: doorways in older apartments are just not made for
tall people. I tell people that when I got to Japan I was two meters tall,

but after hitting my head so many times I took five centimeters off the top. My first house was very old and had doorways so low that I took to wearing my scooter helmet inside the house. At least when I hit my head, which happened on average about once a week, it didn't hurt anymore.

There are bright points to be found in having a small place, however. For one, a small apartment is that much easier to clean. For another, having less space makes one—well me, anyway—more conscious of sorting through what's worth keeping and what's not. I find myself relentlessly paring things down to keep unnecessary clutter at bay.

Japanese housing is described using a combination of numbers (for bedrooms) and letters (L – living room; D – dining room; K – kitchen). So a 1K apartment—the equivalent to a studio apartment—would be a typical single person's apartment, and a 3LDK is generally what a family will live in. A 1R apartment is one room with virtually no attached facilities. Bedrooms may either be Western-style with flooring or Japanese-style with straw mats (*tatami*), or a combination thereof. If it's a Japanese-style room, it will usually—but not always!— comprise six *tatami* and be about 8.5 square meters in size. Western-style rooms, by contrast, will be larger or smaller, depending on the design.

Newer apartments (generally those built in the preceding 10 years) will obviously be much nicer and have more of the latest features than older places. However, quality can still vary—some contractors in the post-bubble era tried to cut corners by using second-rate building materials—so it's worthwhile to know not only the identity of the developer, but also the contractor that actually did the work.

FEATURES OF THE JAPANESE HOME

In addition to the above-mentioned straw mats, the typical Japanese home will have some features that Western homes lack, and vice-versa.

For starters, the entrance of each home will have a hard floor from which one must step up slightly to enter the house. This space, known as the *genkan*, will have an adjacent closet in which to neatly store one's shoes.

There are usually also sliding doors made of paper with a wooden latticework called *shouji*, and solid sliding doors called *fusuma*. Either one of these, or both, will usually be placed at the borders of a Japanese-style room. The room may also feature a small alcove called a *tokonoma*, used for the display of objects d'art, and large closets suitable for storing *futon*. There will inevitably also be some sort of balcony, on which people will hang a rack to dry their clothes.

Except in very cramped apartments, toilets will be located in a room separate from the bath. Modern bathrooms will usually be made of molded plastic seemingly melded together; they're easy to clean but depressingly banal. They permit the bather to shower outside the bath before bathing. Older apartments may still have the old-style bathtubs, in which unheated tap water is filled before starting a gas heater. The heater will circulate the water and warm it up as hot as you can stand it. I honestly prefer this sort of bath and am sorry to see them disappearing from newer housing. The gas handles can be a little tricky to start sometimes, and whatever you do make sure there's lots

This bathroom is designed for Japanese-style bathing:
shower outside the bath, then soak in the tub.

of water in the bath before you crank it up! Modern housing, however, will have a gas water heater that can be turned on and off at will, usually located in the kitchen.

In the kitchen, the stove will likely have two or three burners and a tiny broiler for fish. And that is about the extent of what there is.

What there isn't, of course, is another laundry list. Most notable, probably, is that in Japan apartments are almost always of the unfurnished variety. There seems to be a vast phobia in renting an apartment that contains furniture that might have been used by someone else — even though, as much as people get moved around by their companies like chess pieces, it would be much more sensible and cost-efficient to have furnished apartments.

There are virtually no shared facilities in apartment buildings, either, which means that each person has to buy his own washing machine. If you wish to bake, you'll have to buy a combination microwave oven/conventional oven. Lights too will mostly have to be bought by you, as well as air-conditioners (which function doubly as heat pumps).

Western-style closets may have bars from which to hang clothing, but those bars may be distressingly short and force you to get a supplemental closet. Most problematically of all, many homes simply lack adequate wiring. Too many homes lack the electrical capacity to support the lights, TV, heater, and microwave oven at the same time, and many have been the times I started to make dinner only to have to fumble in the dark and flip the circuit breaker back on. Or there simply may be a lack of outlets; I have been shocked (no pun intended!) to see how many extensions people typically run off of a standard outlet.

JAPANESE FURNITURE

Some furniture and appliances in Japan may be unfamiliar to you. Probably the single biggest difference between Western and Japanese households is the *futon*. Instead of sleeping in a bed with a frame, many people in Japan lay out a *futon*, which is essentially a soft mattress with a quilted covering. Extra blankets can be added in winter for warmth. By day the *futon* can be left on the floor or rolled up and put away. Perhaps once a week you'll see (and hear) house-wives hanging their *futon* out on the balcony on a sunny day and beating them with a small stick to shake out mites. Although the first time I used a *futon* I thought, "Wow! This is just like camping," in time I have grown to prefer them to Western-style beds. In often-cramped Japanese rooms, beds make an annoying obstacle in the middle of the floor. By contrast, *futon* can be readily walked across. Space can be the most valuable commodity of all!

The *kotatsu* is an electric table, which at first thought probably makes as much sense as an electric dog-polisher. But it is a handy way to keep warm during the winter; you can put your legs under the table and warm them up in a hurry. Don't fall asleep under it, though!

Generally, you will find a lot of furniture in the shops to be too small. You will have to hunt around, and pay much more, to find larger tables and chairs.

JAPANESE APPLIANCES AND ELECTRICITY

Rice cookers (*suihanki*) make cooking rice exceptionally easy. Be aware that the rice will be prepared the way your mother told you never to prepare rice, i.e., sticky and glutinous. Most rice cookers will indicate on the pot how much water you should add per cup of rice.

Nothing illustrates better the continuing schisms in Japan than the fact that electricity, which is 100 V throughout, cycles at 50 Hz in eastern Japan and 60 Hz in western Japan. Most, but not all, electric products sold in Japan should be able to function at either setting.

If you bring something from abroad that runs on a slightly different voltage, it might be able to work here. But there's no guarantee it will work just as well when you take it back to your home country. Electrical transformers are available at larger electronics shops.

GARBAGE AND RECYCLING

If you never had to recycle your garbage before, you will certainly learn about it now! Even the smallest town will require you to separate, at the very least, burnable garbage from non-burnable garbage. Generally speaking, burnable garbage will be collected at least twice a week, while non-burnable garbage will be collected perhaps every other week. You will undoubtedly be informed of the schedule when you move into your housing, or when you register at the city hall or ward office; one stop on your "tour" of the office will be at the counter in charge of garbage collection. Very likely you will be handed a paper with easily comprehensible pictures detailing garbage rules.

Depending on your locality, garbage may be further separated into different collection days for glass, plastic drink bottles (known in Japan as PET bottles and stamped as such) with their plastic seal removed, metal containers used for food, metal containers *not* used for food, white Styrofoam used for packaging fresh meats and fish, newspapers, small electronics, and large electronics such as TVs and other bulky items. The latter usually require you to purchase a stamp at a convenience store and paste it on the side of the item, as well as call a recycling center and find out when someone can come by and pick it up. The price of the stamp will vary according to the size of the item.

Hold on—I'm not finished yet. Used batteries should be turned in to an electronics store, which will accept them for recycling. Used computers have different rules; if you are throwing away a computer made by a Japanese manufacturer, the manufacturer is supposed to claim it for recycling, but if it was made by a non-Japanese manufacturer, you will have to contact your municipality for collection. The major exception to that rule, however, is Tokyo, which requires you

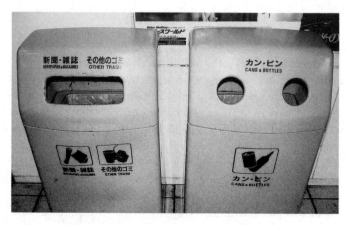

SEPARATE AND EMPTY. *People are usually expected to separate their garbage into burnable and unburnable trash.*

to contact the Japan Electronics and Information Technology Industries Association for collection. Check out the JEITA website (**www.jeita.or.jp/index.htm**) for more information. Or do what I do — simply take your old computer with you on a trip home and throw it away there. (I look forward to the nasty letters criticizing my environmentally unfriendly stance!)

Finally, remember that garbage can only be placed in the appropriate bag; random plastic bags are not OK — a friend of mine did so and was threatened with a 30,000 yen fine! You can buy the correct bags at any supermarket or convenience store.

I have been reassured that all of this garbage is reliably taken care of once the proper authorities collect it; however, I can't help but feel that some of it is being secretly dumped in the sea somewhere. That's just me, I suppose, but even so the "proper" way of disposing with burnable garbage is by, yes, burning it, so just hope that you don't live anywhere near an incinerator. And then people scratch their heads and wonder why the soil in Japan shows such high levels of dioxin ...

HOUSING ISSUES

If you live in a house, be aware that the *genkan* is a sort of quasi-public space. Many guests will not knock on your door but instead will open the door, step inside, and call out to you. I found this out the hard way after taking a shower and then walking through the living room with nothing but a towel. Suddenly I realized that the owner of my house, together with the couple that was going to buy the house, were standing inside the doorway ready to take an unannounced tour of my place. Assuming that you too are the sort of person who is troubled by this, do what I did after that and always lock your door.

Most apartment buildings will have some sort of "leader" who will organize periodic meetings of all the residents, during which issues affecting everyone will be raised and discussed — how to pay for the vandalized elevator, or what to do about pedestrians who insist on cutting across the building's parking lot. You can probably invest an amount of time into these meetings commensurate with the time you expect to live in Japan. Occasionally a circular providing information, both critical and not-so-critical, will be passed around to each dweller; stamp it or sign it and pass it on to the next person.

You may also be approached by your local neighborhood association, known as a *kumiai*, and asked to pay a fee called the *kumiai-hi*. This association is responsible for paying for such things as neighborhood street lights, local festivals, and events for children living in the area. The fee is the same for each household in the area.

By far the biggest housing issue you may confront, however, is the dreaded key money (*shikikin*). The key money is Japan's equivalent of a security deposit. However, unlike Western security deposits which are usually in the neighborhood of one month's rent, key money in Japan will often be in the range of three to seven months' rent. Add to that the rental agency's commission and the first month's rent, and the initial layout for an apartment can be staggering. If you're relocating to Japan in order to begin work, keep in mind that employers — good ones, anyway — will usually offer a short-term, no-interest loan to help you spread the cost of renting your apartment out over a few months.

There is one very, very important fact to keep in mind. When vacating the apartment, Japanese people traditionally have allowed the landlord to keep a portion of the key money — generally around 50 percent! This is nothing but flagrant theft; according to the law, if your apartment shows only general "wear and tear" associated with normal use, *you are entitled to all of your key money back*. The law explicitly says that tenants are not required to pay for the restoration of the apartment, no matter what the actual contract may say.

If you'd like some documentation regarding that point that you'd like to show to your landlord and/or rental agent, go to **http:// annie.ne.jp/~y-s/t/shikikin.htm**. You can print out the relevant documents and show them to your landlord and/or rental agency. In a society that abhors litigation, this is generally enough. Should there be some reluctance on the part of your landlord to return the full amount, you should also take the time to write a follow-up letter, explaining your points. Courts in Japan require written evidence of a problem, and this is one way to buttress your case should you have a serious dispute.

To counter tenants' slow awakening to their rights, some apartment building chains are changing their rules and now require a "membership fee" that is equivalent to the key money rates they previously garnered.

A RACIST SOCIETY?

If there is one aspect of living in Japan which is bound to introduce the foreigner to the racism that some Japanese have, it will manifest itself when you rent an apartment. The "foreigners may be glamorous advertising models but I wouldn't want them living in my apartment" attitude will undoubtedly crop up, and it will take some patience and endurance on your part to get a decent place to live.

My last rented apartment was a case in point. I went to a rental agency with my friend, a Japanese man, who very wisely brought his 1-year-old daughter along on our Saturday visit, thus softening our image in the eyes of the rental agents. They showed us some places, and I decided upon the new three-bedroom apartment they showed me. The following Monday I put down my deposit and signed a contract, and the agent told me I could move in on Saturday.

Friday night I got a phone call from my friend's wife. Suddenly the apartment wasn't available anymore, and the agency was terribly sorry, but would I be interested in moving into any of the other apartments they had available, even though I hadn't seen some of them? I subsequently learned that, although the agents had taken a liking to me, the landlord himself was utterly opposed to a *gaijin* moving in, and had made his opposition known to the agency. The agency found itself doing some last-minute temporizing.

Obviously, I was furious. Worse, I suddenly felt very alone and naked in a faraway land. When you live abroad, there are times when you feel yourself being carried along on clouds generated by the excitement of participating in another culture, and then without warning you crash down to *terra firma* and see the ugliness that was also there all along. This, unfortunately, was one of those times.

Fortunately, though, my friend came through with flying colors. Ignoring the mandatory Friday-night drinking with his colleagues, he paid a late-evening visit to the agency and gave them a rough time, essentially asking, "Why?" The poor agents were caught in the middle, and when my friend pointed out that I had a signed agreement, they had no choice but to go back to the landlord and say "look, the contract has been signed, and there's nothing you can do except live by it." Thus, on Saturday morning, wondering exactly where I was going to be living that Saturday night, the agency called to apologize for the delay and say that everything was ready for my arrival. So in the end, everything worked out well, but I have not forgotten those 12 hours.

Some parts of Japan seem more prone to such rental xenophobia than others (Osaka comes to mind), and others less (possibly Kyushu and Hokkaido); but it can crop up anywhere. Conversely, there are some rental agencies in the larger cities that cater to foreigners by showing properties that have all been previously approved by their landlords. Finding such an agency may take a little asking around, or checking local, English-language publications.

Such treatment in a civil society begs the question, "But how can they do that?" The answer to that question lies in the fact that, while Japan is quick to sign many international treaties protesting nuclear weapons and military action, the country has been woefully slow to adopt U.N. charters or other international conventions safeguarding human rights norms. Even when such agreements are signed, they are often done so without providing a concomitant enforcement mechanism. Thus, in Japan there are many civil laws, but, likely as not, there are no meaningful penalties for breaking them. Housing problems are just one very obvious manifestation of such tolerated racism.

HOLIDAY ACCOMMODATION

If you go traveling around the country, there are of course many options when choosing a place to stay for the night. Hotels have all the same features you'd expect to find at home, with one important exception: no tipping! So when I splurge on a night at a nice hotel, I have to overcome my natural tendency to wrestle with the bellman for my bag and let him take care of it. After all, I will be paying the 15 percent "service charge" at the end of my stay regardless.

Another point to keep in mind is that, particularly in the smaller towns, there is still a lot of trust placed in the hotel's guests. If there's beer in the refrigerator, it's not complimentary—the clerk will ask you at the end of the stay whether you've used the mini-bar, and they will depend on their customers' honesty. More importantly, in this day of "I'm sorry, but if you don't have a credit card we can't accept your reservation," it is perfectly all right to settle your account in cash, often at the end of your stay.

Apart from Western-style hotels, there are a number of options:

- **Business hotels** are scaled-down versions of regular hotels, without all of the frills. They are also cheaper, and are perfect for the solo traveler, businessman or otherwise. The major problem with business hotels is that, since most businessmen are heavy smokers, it can sometimes be difficult to get a nonsmoking room. If that concerns you, do like the British do and ask to see—or in this case, smell— the room first.

  One other quirk to keep in mind about getting a room for the night is that a "single" means a bed that can only hold one person and a "double" means one that can sleep two people. Do not be mistaken in thinking that a "double" is the equivalent of two double beds!

- *Minshuku* are vaguely similar to a B&B. *Minshuku* are where many regular Japanese stay, particularly families on a tight budget. The accommodation is somewhat Spartan: a series of Japanese-style rooms off a corridor, each with a TV and futons and little else. The bathing and toilet facilities are communal, and the overnight charge usually includes breakfast (and some times dinner, too, though if you plan to eat elsewhere you don't have to pay for meals). *Minshuku* can be great for meeting ordinary people in an intimate setting. Learn a few phrases of Japanese and enjoy!

• **Love hotels** are instantly identifiable at night by their gaudy neon lighting; if you see a building lavishly bathed in orange and green hues and it's not a pachinko parlor, it has to be a love hotel. Love hotels are, as the name implies, a place where lovers can duck in for a couple of hours or overnight. However, while the trysting itself may be dubious, these are not sleazy motels **at all**. They are extraordinarily clean and, compared with many business hotels, offer a great deal more value for money.

The hotels are geared for secrecy. A menu at the entrance displays the available rooms; darkened pictures indicate rooms already occupied. Make your selection and take the elevator marked "up" (as opposed to the elevator marked "down" — no need to run into other people on their way out!) After entering the room, the door will automatically lock behind you. Some rooms have automatic meter machines and will calculate your bill when you are ready to leave. In rooms with vacuum tube relays, the telephone will ring and management will ask how long you intend to use the room. A "rest" is usually for two hours and a "stay" is for all night (but usually only from 10 p.m.; if you check in for the night before 10, you will be charged the "stay" fee and some portion of the "rest" fee as well). It is also possible to check in in the early afternoon for an all-aternoon "rest", at least until 5 p.m. For hotels without meters, you will also have to ring when you are ready to leave. Naturally, love hotels do not accept reservations!

• **Capsule hotels** are perhaps the strangest place of all one could wind up sleeping. A capsule hotel will have a locker room (and a small one at that) in which to store one's personal belongings. If there's an attached sauna, you can wash up there and then retire to your capsule, which is—let's face it—a coffin with a light and a TV. It is actually quite comfortable (I suppose my coffin will be, too) although a tall person will find his feet pressing up against the little curtain at the entrance where one climbs into the capsule. Capsule hotels are single-sex only and almost always for men, though there are some capsule hotels for women.

- **Ladies' hotels** are the women's revenge in a decidedly male chauvinistic society. As the name implies, they are for women only, particularly women who can't stand dealing with chain-smokers, heavy drinkers, and accidental stalkers. They are found in most large cities, and they are done up (so I am told) in pastels and sometimes oh-too-cute decorations.
- **Japanese inns** (*ryokan*) are the class of the lot. While some older *ryokan* may appear a little shopworn, most inns are usually lovingly maintained and come with a very high level of service. They can also be very, very expensive! However, a *ryokan* with an attached hot spring is a wonderful experience, perhaps one of the best you can have in Japan.
- **Pensions** are usually Western-inspired inns. They are primarily found in resort areas, and will often be focused on a certain theme in regards to their décor and menu, e.g., a "Swiss" pension will be in the form of a chalet and offer cheese fondue for dinner, etc. Generally speaking, these are less expensive than *ryokan* and make for a delightful getaway option.
- **Temple lodging** (*shukubou*) is available in many places throughout the country for people who would like the opportunity to quietly intermingle with the daily life of Buddhist or Shinto priests. You can find such lodging in places with many active temples, such as Kyoto; the charge is very reasonable.
- **Youth hostels** can be found sprinkled throughout the country.

ENCHANTED FOREST. *Is this what you came looking for? Remote inns next to mountain streams and flanked by tall trees still exist.*

Some of them have a bit of a military atmosphere; others merely feel like extraordinarily cheap *minshuku*. A Japan Youth Hostel membership or an International Youth Hostel Card is of course helpful but not always necessary; many will accept guests without either one. Visit **www.jyh.or.jp/** for more information

• **Gaijin houses** are better seen as midterm accommodation for new arrivals to Japan, but they can also provide an inexpensive place to stay for a few days. Since many new arrivals to Japan are trying very hard to make a few yen go a long way, gaijin house standards usually vary from plain to poor. Check out **www.japan-guide.com/e/e2032.html** for a further explanation and a listing of some gaijin houses.

At this point you might be wondering how to get more information for a weekend in the country. It's easy! Virtually every bookstore will have a selection of glossy magazines devoted only to travel—just look for the ones with vacation-type photos on the cover. Inside you'll find numerous listings about different resorts, grouped according to geographic area. Each listing will have a photo of the resort and a sample meal. Do as the Japanese do and look for something you like, then work out the arrangements and head off on your trip!

Chapter Five

GETTING AROUND

"When I get real bored, I like to drive downtown and get a great parking spot, then sit in my car and count how many people ask me if I'm leaving."

–Comedian Steven Wright

Japan couldn't be a country perpetually in motion unless there was a multitude of ways to get around. There are lots of cars, of course, but there are also other equally worthwhile options for transportation.

PRIVATE CARS

New cars are expensive and should only be considered if you're truly intent on making a big splash among your freshly met acquaintances. If you are, then ignore the Japanese models and go straight for the name-brand value of European cars: A sporty BMW convertible will show that you are a person to be reckoned with, or at least to be taken advantage of. And if your car should qualify for the exclusive "33" or "330" license plates, you're welcome to my parties anytime!

However, if you're like me and 99 percent of my friends, you are probably satisfied in getting any sort of car just to go exploring on your own. Japan has a very large used car market, and there are lots of cars around for good prices. The catch in shopping for cars, however, is in identifying when the infamous car inspection tax, or *shaken* (sounds a bit like "Shockin'!"), will come due on the vehicle. The very expensive car inspection tax is, depending on your point of view, either a noble effort to periodically inspect cars for environmentally damaging emissions, or an underhanded tactic to kick back money to auto repair shops, as well as "encourage" domestic consumption of vehicles. The car inspection tax, you see, is waived for the first three years of a new vehicle's life, and then comes due every two years after. Naturally, older cars will need a lot more "maintenance" than newer cars. It goes a long way to explaining why you don't see old cars on the road in Japan.

So if you're shopping for a new car, pay careful attention to the car inspection tax sticker prominently located on the front windshield beneath the rear-view mirror. One car may be cheaper than another, but if the car inspection tax is coming due that much sooner, it may actually be the worse deal. And though you *could* drive the car without paying the tax, heaven help you should you have an accident and find yourself having to prove that you weren't driving a deathtrap down the road.

You can, if you like, try to do a lot of the car inspection yourself, thereby cutting a large portion of the fee you must pay. Like many things in Japan, the work involved might be trying, but it's not impossible. Check out the information available at the following address: **www.mlit.go.jp/jidosha/kensatoroku/kensa/kns02.htm**. It's written in Japanese, so get a friend to help you.

If you're too cheap to buy a car, you may even find someone

willing to give you a car. This bizarre situation may come about simply because it costs money to dispose of a car at a landfill—it seems that no one buys old cars for parts around here. Someone you know may find it a better bargain to hand it off to you instead. Just make sure you've completed all the paperwork and registered the car in your name before taking possession. I failed to do so, and had to contact my friend back in England for his *inkan,* necessary to complete the transaction before I could consign it to the car graveyard.

You will have to prove to your local government office that you can provide a parking space for your new transportation. (You may also have to prove to yourself whether you've made a good choice in buying a car!) I've got a car, but I would never think of driving it to work; there are better options.

But a car is great for those weekend getaways when you're just dying to see something green. The expressways are expensive, naturally, but at least they are designed with lots of service areas. True, local highways can be prohibitively snarled with traffic, but if you drive smartly you can avoid much of it. On a weekend getaway, we usually leave Friday night instead of Saturday morning, and the volume of traffic is astonishingly different. Sometimes we'll even sleep in the car overnight, without the fear of being mugged in our cars, which many drivers in other countries would have. One of my friends crafted an excellent holiday plan for himself: He drove his small van wherever he wanted to go, and slept in it each night. When morning came, he'd drive to the nearest hot spring or public bath, clean up, and head off to his next destination.

Some Tips Regarding Driving
- Expressways require you to stop at a toll booth and get a ticket, which you will present at the end of your trip and pay the appropriate high toll. (Credit cards are accepted if you don't have enough cash.) However, some tollbooth lanes are marked "ETC" for the automatic toll collection devices installed in some cars. If

your car has such a device, you can use the lane; otherwise, use the other lanes.

- Truck drivers are apparently shocked and upset that they might actually have to share the fast lane with ordinary passenger car drivers. Use caution.

- Never assume that the narrow city street you're driving on must necessarily be a one-way street. You will likely be surprised otherwise.

- Neither should you assume that there is a difference between road directions painted in white and those marked in yellow paint. They have seemingly been painted with whatever color was handy at the time.

- Drivers in Japan will not turn on their headlights in the evening until they absolutely, positively have to. The thinking seems to be, "If the lights don't help me to see, I don't need to turn them on." The fact that headlights might possibly help other drivers to see them is apparently irrelevant.

- You may find yourself approaching a traffic signal which has three green arrows pointing left, straight ahead, and right AND a big red light on at the same time. This has happened to me, and I slammed on my brakes in order to figure out the safest option. The car horn behind me reminded me that, on Japanese roads, the green arrow always takes precedence over the red light. I presume the red light at that particular intersection was for those people who were thinking about going into reverse.

- Generally speaking, damages for traffic accidents are considered to be the responsibility of whoever was driving the larger vehicle, no matter what other factors are involved. This is particularly worth remembering the next time some grandmother shuffling along the roadside suddenly lurches out into your lane without warning.

- Public parking lots usually advertise themselves as "100-yen" parking lots. The catch, of course, is how many minutes (or nanoseconds, as the case may be) you get for 100 yen. Most are automated and lock your car into place a few minutes after you park. To get your car out, go to the centrally located meter, enter the code of your parking space, and pay.

Scooters and Motorcycles

If a car is beyond consideration but you'd still like to get around on your own, consider a scooter. The popular 50-cc scooters do not require any special licenses if you've already been licensed to drive a car. Plus, parking worries become greatly reduced! Just remember that 50-cc scooters, though they can reach 50 kph and above, are legally required to stay within a 30-kph speed limit and to the left of auto traffic. I have been stopped more than once for violating this law, as I have driven my scooter on regular roads in the middle of vehicular traffic, keeping pace with the other cars. Although I politely listen to each police officer's explanation about driving regulations, I can barely repress shouting my certainty that the only sure way to avoid a fatal accident—and little scooters are involved in more than their share of such mishaps—is to position myself where I am safely visible to every driver. One of my friends was involved in such a terrible accident. A car made a sudden left turn in front of her. She went flying over the car and thereafter spent an agonizing stay at a hospital in Japan. That is one ticket on my tour here that I truly do not want punched.

Safety also dictates wearing a more substantial helmet than comes included with the scooter. Such little scooters are not allowed to be on expressways, however. If you want something larger than a 50-cc bike, you will have to have been previously licensed for such a bike in your home country. Otherwise you will have to go through the same sort of ridiculously overpriced driving school that all Japanese have to endure. Be aware, too, that when you take the driving test at the government agency, you may do everything correctly and still not pass. In order to curtail motorcycle hooliganism, the government tacitly encourages a sort of unofficial quota on how many motorcycle licenses can be issued, especially for the largest bikes. A friend of mine conscientiously prepped for the exam so he could go cruising on his new Harley. He took the test *six* times and failed each time. Frustrated, he wound up screaming at the instructor, who admitted he'd been misleading him as to how to correctly answer the test. On his seventh try, my friend suddenly passed.

The same is true, to a lesser extent, for motorists who apply for a Japanese car license. Drivers from countries that drive on the left-hand side of the road as in Japan are licensed more easily than drivers from other countries (read "the U.S.") Considering the number of traffic fatalities caused by careless American servicemen, especially in Okinawa, it seems Japanese prudence might be justified.

Bicycles

Bicycles are popular in those cities that are sited on predominantly flat land. In Japan you don't need a powerful mountain bike or a hot racing bike—those little "granny" bikes are favored by everyone, and are more comfortable, too. Bicycles can be ridden on either streets or sidewalks (unless otherwise posted), and though pedestrians may find the whirring bicycles annoying, one look at the streets, tightly packed with cars, will help you understand why the bicyclists prefer the sidewalks.

Bicycles are parked anywhere, although they really shouldn't be as they cause a spectacular mess on the sidewalks. For a modest fee there are public parking spaces for bikes—you just have to hunt around to find them. If there isn't such a place nearby, go ahead and lock your bike up. However, you will find your bike is much safer if you lock it with a U-lock instead of the chintzy little lock that comes with the bike, and safest of all if you lock the bike to something stationary. People who tell you that there is no theft in Japan obviously never owned a bicycle or an umbrella.

Walking

In all likelihood, you will be walking much more in Japan than you ever did in your hometown. So many things will be packed into a small area, plus the streets will be generally more conducive to walking, that you'll find it one of the easiest ways to appreciate the country.

Some things to keep in mind: As noted before, bikes are allowed on sidewalks unless prohibited by signs. If you, the pedestrian, suddenly veer in another direction, take a discrete look over your shoulder and make sure you don't collide with a cyclist.

Second, while the government may have done much for its vision-impaired citizens by installing special sidewalk markers and chirping street signals, it is shockingly deficient in making life easier for wheelchair-bound people. Japan, as you will quickly discover, is full of steps and stairs. A person needs to be reasonably fit in order to navigate the maze of pedestrian bridges, tunnels, detours, and slopes. The average Japanese in his lifetime will endure more steps than a convention full of recovering alcoholics; he will suffer through more stairways than a Led Zeppelin groupie.

Third, be aware that a lot of stones used in paving sidewalks and building entrances have a glossy finish. When compounded with a rainy day and leather soles, walking can be a treacherous activity. Be careful!

Last, you may find that while walking you are prepared to give way 50 percent of the time and expect people to give way the other 50 percent, in Japan it often feels like everyone is involved in a game of "pedestrian chicken". When two people meet at right angles, it seems that they both accelerate in an attempt to cut the other person off. And when they meet from opposing directions, "there can be only one!"

SUBWAY, TRAIN, AND MONORAIL

The major cities of Japan (Tokyo, Yokohama, Sapporo, Sendai, Nagoya, Fukuoka, Osaka, Kyoto, and Kobe) all have subways, and many of them have extensive commuter train networks, together with the occasional monorail, as well. There probably isn't any map in this world more intimidating, initially, than the rail map for the city of Tokyo, which resembles nothing so much as a plate of spaghetti dumped on the floor. Then you go through stations that are operated by different private companies and connected willy-nilly with a maze of stairs, hurtling headlong with 27,348 commuters making the same transfer, and you realize it truly *is* intimidating.

Fear not! Veteran Japan hand that I am, I will pass along my trade secret as to how to cope with the crush of people and retain your sanity: *Go back home*. If you can't do that, however, then just buy your ticket, hold your breath, and jump in. Actually, riding the trains in Tokyo is not unpleasant in the middle of the day, and even on the well-traveled Yamanote line you can sometimes get a seat.

But the mornings and evenings can be a struggle, and yes, Virginia, they do have subway "packers" to squeeze more people onto the trains. If you're going to live and work in the Tokyo or Osaka areas, you had better quickly ascertain whether a) your job is near your home, or b) you can endure the train rides to and fro. If the answer is "no" to both, then it is exceedingly likely that you will be very, very miserable.

To buy a ticket, look for your destination on the board above the ticket vending machines, then put your money into the machine and punch the button for the appropriate fare. If you make a mistake in the ticket you buy, present it to the stationmaster before you pass through the electronic ticket gate and you can easily get a refund. As you pass through the gate, the ticket will be returned to you. Keep the ticket with you until the end of your journey and pass it through the wicket at the end of your trip. As one might guess, it's not a good idea to lose your ticket during your journey.

If you are a regular commuter, you can buy a pass (*teiki*) for a period of a month or more. Students are eligible for deeply discounted passes. Alternatively, you can buy plastic transportation cards with a certain stored value; these cards will often give you 10 to 18 percent more in value than their original purchase price. You can use these cards either as regular tickets, or at the ticket machines to purchase ordinary tickets.

Trains will be entirely nonsmoking. In addition, some train lines offer women-only cars (usually to be seen during morning rush hours) to provide relief from the legendary groping men of Japan's crowded trains.

JR Train Network

Originally just one company, the excellent Japan Railways network was split up into a number of regional entities. Though some people use JR as a commuter line, it primarily functions as a collection of long-distance trains that crisscross the country. Local trains that make every stop are called *futsuu*, limited-express trains are called *tokkyuu*, and express trains in the middle of those two are called *kaisoku*. Outside of major metropolitan areas you will only find local and limited express trains. Local and express trains cost the same to the same destination, but limited express trains require an additional, and rather hefty, express surcharge. There are also overnight sleeper trains between faraway destinations. JR trains have both smoking and nonsmoking cars, and both reserved and non-reserved cars. Reservations can add a bit to the ticket price but can be very well worth it during holiday periods (read: New Year's, Golden Week, and o-bon!)

There are sometimes special deals and programs for two people traveling together; however, there are very few discounts available for the single traveler. The Japan Rail Pass, sold overseas, can be used only by tourists to Japan. The one cheap rail possibility for Japan residents is the *seishun jyuhachi kippu*. Originally intended for students but certainly not limited to them, the *seishun jyuhachi kippu* is a package of five tickets, each one for unlimited rail travel on local or express trains only. The tickets will only be valid during student holiday periods, e.g., spring or summer. But if you've got the time and some good books for the journey, it can still be a fun way to get around.

FASTER THAN A SPEEDING ... *A bullet train whips through a station.*

JR has so many stations that, in the sticks, the "station" is nothing more than a rough platform and a small shelter from the elements. In such rural areas the stations work on the honor system; tell the conductor where you got on and where you're traveling to, and he'll give you the appropriate ticket. And when getting off the train at stations without automatic wickets, just drop your ticket in the little box with a slot near the exit.

Bullet Train

The bullet trains are incredibly fast and should be experienced at least once. Known as *shinkansen*, the train lines connect the major cities of Honshu, and are now being expanded to include Kyushu as well. The trains are certainly more exciting for non-Japanese; most Japanese just think, "It's a fast train — so what?"

Bullet trains will have an entrance and exit separate from regular JR trains. You can often use bullet train tickets for immediate travel beyond the bullet train station, i.e., once you get off the bullet train at Point X, you might be able to use the local trains to go a couple of stations down the way. Inquire first.

City Bus

City buses are more daunting initially than the subways and commuter trains. At least with the latter two you have some time to examine a map (nearly always including English or Romanized lettering), then take another moment to consider which platform to plop yourself onto. With a bus, however, you might be sitting at a bus stop as buses come racing one after another, with signs that might only be written in Japanese, and you have perhaps two seconds to decide whether to jump onto it. ("This one? Maybe? No. Yes! No! …Wait!")

Get your destination written down in Japanese and either pick out the correct bus by recognizing some of the easier kanji, or enlist the services of a sympathetic bystander to help you catch the right bus. You can also ask the bus driver, of course.

Some buses require you to enter through the front door and some through the back; watch what other people do and enter with them. Some buses require you to pay upon entering, others require you to grab the little paper ticket sticking out from a machine found just inside the door. This ticket will be marked with a number, which will match a display located above the driver. Below your number you will see the fare in Japanese yen. When you get to your stop, drop the ticket and the correct change into the box next to the driver and get off through the front door.

When you want to get off, push one of the buttons found on the side or the ceiling, and the driver will let you off at the next stop. Also, if you need to make change, you can usually change coins, or a 1,000-yen note, at an automatic coin changer at the front of the bus. The machines do not change larger bills; if all you've got is a 10,000-yen note, the driver will have to grumpily use his microphone to ask the other passengers if there is anyone who can change money for you. Upon getting your change in coins, quickly proceed to insert the exact amount into the machine.

As with trains and subways, you can also purchase commuter passes, student passes, or discounted prepaid cards.

Highway Bus

Japan is connected from end to drivable end by a network of highway buses. These are operated in a manner similar to city buses, but if there is a vending machine at the bus station you are expected to pay for your ticket before boarding. A one-way ticket is called *katamichi*; a return ticket (usually slightly discounted) is called *oufuku kippu*.

There are overnight buses that provide reasonably comfortable sleeping. Complimentary tea or coffee is sometimes available. Some buses will have an onboard toilet; those that don't will ensure a five-minute rest stop about every two hours or so. Don't wander off and let the bus leave you!

Streetcar

In the bigger cities of Japan, streetcars have sadly disappeared. However, they are still found in the smaller cities at either end of the country (e.g., Hakodate, Matsuyama, Hiroshima, Nagasaki, Kumamoto, and Kagoshima.) Most of the streetcars work on the same principle as the buses; pay according to how far you have traveled. Nagasaki's is unique, however, in that it is 100 yen regardless of distance—a great bargain for a narrow, lengthy city. Just don't bump your head on all the overhanging advertisements.

Taxi

This isn't New York City—the taxis here are clean! Taxis invariably come with spotless white seat covers, doilies decorating the head-rests, and a bottle of air freshener behind the back seat. Moreover, the drivers all still wear caps and white kid gloves. And you don't even have to open the door yourself—the driver opens the rear left door via a remote handle!

Taxis are a great help in finding that particular place you'd never be able to locate yourself, although it may even be a little tricky for the driver himself. You may see him simultaneously study a map, consult with his dispatcher by two-way radio, and still weave through traffic at hair-raising speed with nonchalant grace. The good point is that, like everywhere else in Japan, you don't have to tip unless you have truly put your driver through an inordinate amount of grief—and even then it will likely be refused. The bad point is that, though no-smoking rules are in place for most taxis, you may still jump inside one that smells like yesterday's ashtray.

When hailing a taxi, a taxi with a red light in the front window means that it is free. A green light means that it is taken. (No, I can't explain it, either.) A yellow light means that it is on call.

Though incidents regarding drivers taking their passengers "for a ride" are exceedingly rare, they are not unknown. As we approached the port one night, the driver flicked off the true taxi meter located under the radio, but the digital meter on the dashboard was still running. When we arrived, he gestured at the dashboard meter. I merely asked for a receipt—printed out by the bottommost meter— then feigned incredulous shock that, somehow, the two figures could be different. Needless to say, the driver was humiliated to be caught.

FERRY, JETFOIL, AND SPEEDBOAT

Japan, of course, has lots of islands and you may find yourself heading out to one. Alternatively, if you've got the time to kill, long-distance ferries are great for getting around the main islands themselves— considering the distance covered, prices for these ferries are ridicu-lously low for travelers *sans* automobiles.

Ferries are the cheapest sea voyage option. Many require you to fill out a little form beforehand listing your name, age, and address. This is obviously in case there is an accident and the company must notify the next-of-kin. I must admit to taking all of that documentation rather cavalierly and writing in someone else's name; if the ship were to sink, I at least would have the morbid satisfaction of envisioning the next day's news headline: MICHAEL JORDAN DROWNS IN JAPAN FERRY DISASTER. Practically speaking, ferries in Japan are not prone to the sorts of accidents you read about in other parts of Asia. The number of passengers will be limited, and in rough weather they simply don't go.

Usually you will hand over a boarding pass when you get on and the ticket itself when you get off. The boarding pass is numbered so that people can get on the ferry in the order that they purchased tickets. If you're taking a car or bike aboard, be sure to arrive in plenty of time to load your vehicle. And if you suffer from seasickness, the best tip is to simply lie down.

Speedboats are naturally faster, but they can be a bit rougher as they crash into wave after wave. Jetfoils are the smoothest (and most expensive) option; a ride aboard one is like riding a wave-cropping airplane.

Nothing illustrates the Japanese public sense of taking care of the group than my attempt to get on a ferry one Sunday. Upon being asked by my friend as to what time the ferry departed, I rather casually answered, "Around one, I think." We arrived at the port at exactly one o'clock, and I confidently noted that, yes, the ferry was still there. Then I did a double take and saw that the ferry's back door, through which cars were loaded, was shut. Worse, the boat was churning water and beginning to move.

I jumped out of my friend's car, slung my backpack over my shoulders, and dashed down the dock. I cut through the waiting area and, with *Indiana Jones*-style trumpets blaring inside my head, grabbed hold of an iron railing and slung myself underneath it. Unfortunately, weighted down with the backpack, I crashed on my back like a turtle. Scrambling back up, I ran alongside the boat and bellowed for them to please wait. (*"Chotto matte, kudasai!"*)

The boat was two meters away from the dock, and one last rope was just waiting to be cast off. In any other country, that would have

been it for me. "Good luck making the next one!" is what I would have heard, I'm sure. But the crew of this particular boat proceeded to back the ferry closer to the dock, opened the portal and laid out a flimsy emergency ramp for me to board the craft. I tried to thank someone onboard, but whom do you thank when everyone ignores you and goes about their business like it is a typical day for them?

AIRPLANE

Air routes knit the country together from one end to the other. Two major carriers (Japan Airlines and All Nippon Airways) and several regional carriers will fly to even the remotest islands. The link between Tokyo and Fukuoka is the busiest in the world, and increased competition often means that an air ticket will be cheaper than the equivalent rail ticket.

Because the country is so small and flights so short, there is almost no in-flight meal service. However, even the smallest airport will have a restaurant, and the bigger airports will have numerous restaurants that serve satisfyingly delicious and healthy meals. For the frequent commuter, there are ticket vending machines similar to those at train stations—just buy a ticket and go.

Hitchhiking

No author today would recommend hitchhiking—at least not one without a good lawyer ready at his side! So with that in mind, I'm certainly not going to do so.

What I will say, however, is that I have hitched to many, many places in Japan, and have never been shown anything except overwhelming kindness and generosity by the people who gave me rides. Typically I've waited no more than five minutes before someone stopped, usually explaining that "Japanese people never hitchhike. If I hadn't stopped, you would never have gotten a ride." People have invariably given me presents—a can of beer, a dinner at a service area, a toy teddy bear. All they expected in return was that I be an entertaining companion to pass the miles. It introduced me to an impressive cross-section of society, and it certainly gave my language skills a bit of a workout.

Camel

OK, so I'm fudging a bit on this one, but if you visit the famous (in Japan, anyway) sand dunes of Tottori prefecture, you can pretend you're Lawrence of Arabia and ride a camel around in a circle. Of course it's touristy and doesn't get you anywhere, but at least you can say you have done it.

Chapter Six

SHOPPING AND SERVICES

"When it is a question of money, everybody is of the same religion."

–Voltaire

No matter where you go with your money in Japan, you will undoubtedly find a much larger shop staff to help you than you would ever expect to find at home. Whether all of these staff members will be able to provide you with a level of service above and beyond a simple cash transaction, however, is questionable.

BANKING

My doctor told me that my blood pressure was running a bit low, and that I should try to do something about it. So I decided to visit a Japanese bank.

Think I'm joking? I went into a bank once exactly at 9 a.m., just as the doors were being opened, merely to break some bills. I stood in front of the teller and explained what I wanted, and (still being groggy at that hour) could not begin to understand what the teller was frantically begging me to do. Finally, what she was saying registered in my brain: "You've got to take a number! You've got to get a ticket!"

I looked around. There was *no one else* in the bank.

What could I do? I followed the rules, took a number, and sat down to wait. *Ping!* "Number One."

"*Hai!*" I boomed.

Because banks deal in big amounts of money, rules are followed even more scrupulously in a country already maniacally excessive about rules. I once was told to fill out a withdrawal slip once more because I'd written "P. SEAN BRAMBLE" on the slip and the bank book read "P. Sean Bramble". "But it's the same thing!" I fruitlessly protested. I wanted my money; I followed the rules.

Things take time to resolve at banks in Japan, which is why people in your office can legitimately disappear for an hour or two with the excuse that they're "at the bank". Not that the banks make people stand for the entire time, thank goodness. When your number is finally called, you approach the teller and explain your transaction, and nine times out of 10 you can take a seat until the teller calls you back to complete the transaction. Enjoy the magazines.

Most people make do with only an ordinary savings account (*futsuu yokin*). To open an account, you will need to show identification; however, an *inkan* or *hanko* are not necessary to authorize a withdrawal, as banks will also accept signatures these days. At some banks you will receive a little bank book and, if you so desire, an ATM card. Other banks are starting to move away from the passbook era

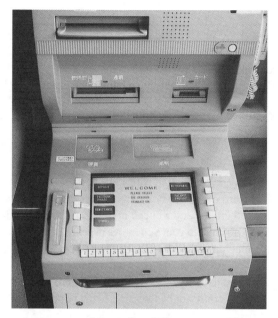

NEED MONEY? *Post office ATMs are accessible throughout Japan, accept coins or bills for deposit, and have English instructions.*

and instead are providing their customers with monthly statements — Shinsei Bank is one such bank. Most banks have reciprocal agreements with other banks and permit customers to use ATMs of different banks for withdrawals, but some of them will charge for the privilege and others won't; inquire first.

Note that there is no such thing in Japan as a joint savings account. Accounts must be opened in one person's name only. It sounds restrictive but it really isn't; our bank provides us with both a passbook (which can be inserted into an ATM and used like an ATM card) and an ATM card. I've got the bank book; my wife's got the ATM card.

Although it is theoretically possible to open a checking account at some banks, it is really not worth it. Most people in Japan have never even seen a personal check and can't conceive how you could possibly pay a bill, let alone the pizza delivery guy, with a small piece of paper you've just filled out. Instead, most people in Japan keep a smattering of bank books to pay this or that bill at different banks; people spend a lot of time walking around trying to complete their transactions. Most businesses, meanwhile, will open a current account at the bank and advise their customers of their account information. If you ask your bank to process a check you receive from abroad, you may be confronted with some hefty fees. I gave up asking my British health insurance company to recompense me in yen and instead asked them to send a check in dollars to my account abroad.

If you need to change your yen into different denominations, some banks have machines that only make change (*ryougae*). Open until 3 p.m., the machines should be fairly self-explanatory, but you can ask for help if you need it. Also, in a nod to incomprehensible rules, the hours for deposits may not be the same as the hours for withdrawals.

Which bank should you choose when setting up your account? Well, that will depend largely upon two factors: which bank is convenient to both your home and workplace, and which bank can accept deposits from your company. Although companies can deposit your pay into virtually any account, some companies are still restricted from putting money into post office accounts.

Despite that, I still think that the post office bank offers the best bank accounts overall. First, the interest rate is almost always better than that available from a commercial bank (although the difference in an age of deflation can truly be infinitesimal!) Second, post office ATMs usually have better hours than do commercial banks. Third, unlike commercial banks, there is no charge whatsoever for weekend, or late-night, or holiday withdrawals. My friend was in dire straits one weekend and needed the 1,000 yen left in his commercial bank account—but couldn't withdraw it because he didn't have enough in the account to cover the 105 yen service fee.

Fourth, and perhaps most importantly if you intend to see much of the country, you can find a post office ATM almost anywhere in the country. No bank has a comparable reach, particularly into the outlying areas of Japan.

If you've got some banking to take care of and you want to avoid long lines, try not to go to the bank between 1 and 2 p.m. (payments made after 2 p.m. are generally recorded the following business day) or on payday (the 25th is people's most common payday; the 21st is also popular). And stay far away in the few days just before the New Year's holiday if you can—the bank is full of grandparents withdrawing money to give as New Year's presents to their grandchildren.

It is very important to note that, just because an ATM booth may sport stickers of every credit card you've ever heard of, and dozens more you haven't, it does NOT mean that you can use your foreign-issued credit card to withdraw a cash advance against your credit line. Maybe 98 percent of such ATMs are strictly for cards issued in Japan; if you find an ATM that accepts your overseas-issued card, chances are it will be near a major train station or airport. Make sure you get your money before you really need it—if necessary, visit a bank during normal working hours. Bring a book to read.

MONEY

The currency of Japan is the yen (円 or ¥). Bills come in denominations of 10,000; 5,000; 2,000; and 1,000 yen, although the 2,000-yen note is rare unless you specifically go to a bank and request one. Coins come in denominations of 500, 100, 50, 10, five, and one yen. The 50-yen and five-yen coins have holes in them. The 500-yen coin was recently changed, so some vending machines will only accept the old coins, some will only accept the new ones, and some will accept both.

While some places in Okinawa and cities near U.S. military bases may take U.S. dollars, remember that this is a different country and that there is a different currency in use.

Paying Bills and Sending Money

Utility bills and other payments can be paid at the post office, at banks, and at branches of major convenience store chains. You can also, if you like, arrange for automatic payment of your bills from your bank account, such as your gas, electricity, telephone, and cell phone bills. The good thing about this of course is that it saves you making so many outside trips. The downside, obviously, is that you are granting those companies access to your bank account before you've had time to inspect the bill yourself. Mistakes do happen; Mizuho Bank, formed by the merger of four other banks, launched a new computer system without any testing whatsoever, and within a week it found problems with bill payments. And make sure you read my warning in the chapter about cell phones!

Bills paid directly into a particular bank's ATMs may be charged less of a service fee than bills paid at the bank's counter. Most banks' ATMs do not have English instructions, however, so if you wish to pay through the ATM the best advice is to look utterly lost and get a bank representative (who is always standing nearby) to help you through the whole procedure. ATMs that accept bill payments close at 3 p.m.

If you need to send money abroad to pay a bill, there are a couple of options. One option, of course, is by a bank wire (*denshin soukin*). For large amounts of money, this is the safest and easiest option. You can make arrangements with your own bank; you can also try the services offered by Lloyds TSB Bank at (03) 3589-7745.

Another choice is by international postal money order (*kokusai kawase*). This is probably better for smaller amounts, plus it has the advantage of being available throughout the country via the post office network. You may find yourself burdened by having to fill out so many forms; however, if you often send money to one particular company or person, you can arrange to have a little card made up with the information encoded within.

Since personal checks are virtually unheard of and are more

trouble than they are worth, what do you do when you need to send money to someone in Japan? One way is via domestic postal money orders (*yuubin kawase*), or you could use the cash registration envelope, a special envelope for cash delivery.

POSTAL SERVICES

The postal service, in my eyes, is damn good at what it does. It had better be that good; it certainly costs enough.

Mail is delivered once daily, and despite the fact that Japanese bemoan how long regular delivery takes, I think it moves along smartly. Most people in Japan have letterboxes at the entrance of their apartment buildings which can be accessed by a combination lock, and which also holds not only delivered mail but also all sorts of junk mail that passing delivery people will shove into your box. Junk mail deliveries can accumulate rapidly; if you plan to take a holiday, you may want someone to clean out your box if you're going to be gone for an extended period of time.

If you return home and find that the mailman couldn't squeeze your long-awaited package from home into your letterbox, there will be a postcard left in your box asking you to telephone the post office within a few days. You can then make arrangements for the post office to deliver the package to your door within a certain time frame, usually a week.

To send mail, just look for the red mail boxes liberally scattered throughout the country. The post office's symbol looks like the letter "T" with an extra horizontal bar above the "T"; the symbol is also placed just before the postal code on envelopes.

Prices change relatively slowly in Japan, so it is with some confidence that I tell you the following prices: domestic postcards, 50 yen; international postcards, 70 yen; domestic letters, 80 yen for the first 25 grams; aerogrammes, 90 yen; and international letters (up to 25 grams), 90 yen to Asia, 130 yen to Africa and South America, and 110 yen to just about everywhere else.

There are other services available, which you can read about in an English handbook called the Post Office Guide. It is available at larger post office branches.

SHOPPING

Over the years, I've learned that "shopping" is people's No. 2 hobby in Japan, right above "driving" and just below "sleeping". (I gave up trying to point out that sleeping doesn't exactly qualify as a hobby.) So if someone in Japan is participating in his favorite activity and he's not snoring, chances are he's in a store somewhere.

Major department stores and electronics stores are particularly notable for the large number of staffers on hand. This is a welcome relief from some other countries where you are either a) forced to wait behind one other customer because the store is so cheap that it will have one employee overseeing three different counters, or b) made to do everything yourself—undoubtedly the day is coming when some smart businessman is going to say, "We could save a lot more money if our customers could just pump the oil out of the ground by themselves." In Japan's biggest stores, you will find clerks clustered around just waiting for you, although be warned that they are not terribly proactive; nobody works on commission here!

In the department stores, there will be fashionably uniformed women who will courteously bow as you enter; at the electronics stores, there will be many men shouting "*Irasshai!*" ("Welcome!") at the tops of their voices or into megaphones. The real problem, though, isn't their manners or volume—it's their competence. A lot of shop employees are surprisingly unable to tell you very much about the products on display. It's not a language issue; it's a case where a lot of temporary help hasn't been properly trained. With my college stereo days far behind me I am hardly on the cutting edge of technology anymore, but more than once I've asked the salesman, "It works like this, doesn't it?" and found him absolutely *relieved* that the customer could figure out the product by himself.

Houston, we have a problem. *No, it's not a real space shuttle, just another example of advertising, Japanese style.*

Bargaining, at least as practiced in other parts of Asia, doesn't really exist here. My friend once visited a secondhand shop and tried to bargain for a sword he saw on display. "It's a little expensive, isn't it," he commented after hearing the price—whereupon the shopkeeper became so incensed that he turned around and refused to deal with him anymore.

You can "bargain" at some trendy electronics quarters, such as Akihabara in Tokyo. However, it would seem that even the "bargain" prices have been pre-determined; haggling at those shops goes something like this:

CUSTOMER: How much is this item?
CLERK: (*attacking the calculator*) 10,000 yen.
CUSTOMER: Please give me a discount.
CLERK: (*attacking the calculator once more*) 9,000 yen.
CUSTOMER: OK.

"Shopping roads" such as this are protected from the rain but leak air conditioning from every shop.

You can bargain a bit for the display item—that is, if they'll let you. One clerk wouldn't let me buy the shop's last available video camera, even though I was perfectly willing to buy the display model. Feigning surprise, I asked, "Is this a shop or a museum?" Suddenly it dawned on him that his job was to move merchandise, not dust it.

The amount of packaging that accompanies your item, whether it's a gift or simply a routine purchase, can be a) beautiful b) annoying, or c) an eye-opening illustration of the mountainous waste that Japan thoughtlessly creates. You can avoid the unnecessary bag for one item by saying "*Sono mama*" ("Just as it is").

If you use a credit card for a large purchase (which can be done in most any large shop) the clerk may ask you over how many months you would like to spread the payments. This is because Japanese credit cards don't operate on a system of revolving credit; customers must decide at the time of purchase as to the number of payments. For holders of overseas-issued cards it doesn't really matter—you can just gesture with one index finger and work it out later yourself.

Bear in mind that clerks are very solicitous of you, at least until you've paid. Should you have any reason to return your merchandise for exchange or refund, make sure you do so within a week at most. Consumer protection laws are virtually nonexistent, and you will need the receipt and original packing, as well as a polite stubbornness, in order to get things resolved to your satisfaction.

I don't know where else to fit this, but one little oddity about shops in Japan is that most of them have doors that open only inward. This is presumably because many shops front directly onto the sidewalk or street, and a door that opened outward would just whack into passersby. Likewise, there may be six glass doors leading into a department store, but only two which are actually unlocked. It is scary to think what would happen if a fire broke out inside the shop.

POINT CARDS

Every shop these days has a point card. Point cards give you points for items you've purchased at the store. If you collect enough points, you can redeem them for free items or discounts on future purchases. I used to like them, but when I saw how quickly my wallet was becoming burdened, I gave up on them.

MARKETS, SUPER AND OTHERWISE

Markets can range from small mom-and-pop operations to the shiniest, biggest chains. The biggest supermarkets may still be smaller than the ones you're used to, but they do manage to cram a lot of things inside them regardless. The two biggest drawbacks are that they generally don't accept anything except cash, and worse, it seems that nobody's ever heard of an express lane for shoppers with only a few items to purchase.

If you only buy one or two items, the clerk will often bag them for you. Otherwise, be prepared to bag everything yourself at the table adjacent to the checkout counter. Although a few extra plastic bags around the house can be useful, you can cut down on the number of bags that you will inevitably go through during the year by purchasing a reusable cloth shopping bag, usually available for sale at large supermarkets. There are no deposits on bottles or cans.

Foods are packaged in smaller amounts than you are likely used to. Milk and juices come in one-liter packages, and bread will usually have only six slices per bag. Also, fruit and vegetables will be sold as presented; breaking those bananas apart and hoping to pay for them by the gram is only going to cause grief. Some fruits in particular will only be available seasonally; strawberry season runs roughly from December to May and is then followed by melon season.

Though the packaging for many things can seem excessive (does each cookie *really* have to be wrapped?) the one good thing in its favor is that it prevents food from wilting during the humid Japanese summer.

Some things you might hope to find at your corner grocery will undoubtedly be lacking and can only be found at larger stores or specialty shops. These may include good bread, sandwich meats other than ham, good cheeses other than camembert, fluoride toothpaste, and anti-perspirant/deodorant. For more "exotic" food items, visit the food department of a large department store, or check to see if there is an import shop in your area.

The American chain Costco has opened some shops in Japan and offers bulk amounts of goods at very reasonable prices. Another option for those who live in remote areas is the Foreign Buyers' Club, which provides customers with the option of catalog shopping for imported American goods; check out **www.fbcusa.com** for more information. Vegetarians and people interested in organic foods may want to visit the Alishan Organic Center at **www.alishan-organic-center.com**.

For items such as fruits, vegetables, fish, and meat, try visiting one of the local shops that seemingly line every little shopping road (*shoutengai*) in Japan. Unlike, say, China, foreigners are not charged any differently than Japanese, and while the prices may sometimes not be any cheaper than the supermarket, you can feel that you are directly involved in supporting the livelihood of small business people, rather than feeding a large corporation.

Co-ops

Co-ops are an alternative to making your way to the supermarket. On a weekly basis they provide a catalog of foods that can be delivered to your home. The catalog will include both daily staples (milk, yogurt, etc.) and seasonal specials. Delivery will be made to your door at a certain time each week, and the delivery man will take away the Styrofoam boxes and crates to use the next time.

Co-ops maintain close relations to their producers, and many co-op products are reputed to be more natural and less insecticide-filled than typical supermarket products. Moreover, co-ops can be cheaper even despite home delivery. They are very popular with housewives, especially those with children. You can get more information about Green Co-op, F Co-op, A Co-op, or others by visiting their supermarkets, or by taking a look at their Japanese web pages.

Convenience Stores

Some parts of Japan have no convenience stores, which is like saying some parts of David Beckham remain unexposed. Convenience stores, most of them open 24 hours, can be found down every street in every city. They may or may not sell alcohol, depending on whether there are bars nearby, but they will have all the expected features of convenience stores around the world.

Convenience stores are also one of the most common destinations for people who step out to get lunch. Around noon the stores offer a large selection of boxed lunches, sandwiches, and instant noodles. The clerks will ask you if you want your lunch warmed in the microwave oven and supply you with chopsticks or fork and spoon.

Hot water thermoses are available for instant noodles. And though I really don't want to be in the position of recommending one chain over another, it does seem that 7-Eleven consistently makes better lunches than its competitors.

Vending Machines

To cut out the legendary middlemen of Japan—or perhaps to spare their customers any embarrassment—many businesses have resorted to offering their products via vending machines. Soft drinks, cigarettes and beer are the most common, but there are also machines dispensing transportation passes, snacks, cup ramen, disposable cameras, eggs, rice, and even condoms—the last packaged for customers' different blood types.

CONSUMPTION TAX

A consumption tax of five percent is charged on everything, including (most shockingly) unprepared food. Since April 2004 the law has mandated that this tax be included in the sticker price of all goods sold at all but the tiniest shops. This is presumably so that people will be less aware of it; it will also make it easier to slip a long-rumored tax increase past the consumer in the near future.

TOILETS

The so-called Japanese toilet is a porcelain version of the hole in the ground, over which one squats. I know quite a few non-Japanese who will go to great lengths to avoid ever having to use them. Personally, I can't really understand why. They are not terribly difficult to use, and since no bare part of one's body ever touches anything, it is impossible to find another toilet that could be more sanitary. Or, to put it another way, if I had a choice between using a Western or Japanese toilet at a New York bus station, I would choose the Japanese toilet every time. The only drawback to a Japanese toilet is that, if you spend

more than a few minutes using one, you may find yourself losing any feeling from your knees down while you are so balanced.

The important thing to remember when using a Japanese toilet is to face the hooded end. Put one foot on each side of the toilet, drop your pants around your ankles, and hunker down. It is also important to remember not to balance forward on the balls of your feet — you're not trying to be baseball catcher Johnny Bench — but rather to lean back on your heels. I think there's a terrific fear on the part of every Westerner who uses a Japanese toilet for the first time that somehow they're going to miss the toilet and hit their clothes instead, but it doesn't happen if you squat correctly.

For those who still cannot overcome their reluctance to use a Japanese toilet, be reassured that most hotels, restaurants, and housing will have Western-style toilets. And it is with these that Japanese creativity runs amok. Toilets at home are just toilets; here, some are veritable rocket ships.

Some toilets will have heated seats, a wonderful winter antidote to a frosty morning's wake-up call. Others will be equipped with various water sprays for cleaning, and a warm air fan for drying. Still others will emit a deodorizing fragrance from time to time. One toilet I saw in a hotel was equipped with a superior sanitary touch; a mechanical device would roll out a paper seat cover at the press of a button. And, to counteract people's (particularly women's) wasteful tendency to constantly flush in order to cover up any disquieting sounds, some toilet stalls come equipped with noisemakers on the wall that, at the push of a button, will simulate the sound of running water.

To explain all of this high-tech wizardry, many toilets will have instructions (in Japanese, of course) explaining what to do — even sometimes down to the comical pictographs explaining to people from the backcountry not to stand on the toilet seat, but rather to sit down upon the seat itself. City dwellers may snicker, but they serve a real purpose; there's a good many folks in the country who have never had anything at home apart from a "long drop".

Many toilets are even designed to fill the tank via a small tap, which can also double for washing your hands. That's the good side of water conservation; the bad is that most every toilet uses very little water. Should you need it, there will always be a toilet brush nearby, if you get my drift.

Countering all of this attention to detail is that some public facilities — not all, but some — will be without any paper whatsoever. Prudence dictates that you always keep a little mini pack of tissues on your person, just in case. And a puzzling postscript to all of this is that, while some washrooms may come equipped with hand soap and others will have paper towels or a hand blow dryer, it is all but impossible to find the washroom which has both — if you find one, write down the address and tell your friends. If you wonder why Japanese people are not forever wiping their hands on their pants as they walk out of the washroom, keep in mind that they always have a handkerchief with them.

–Chapter Seven–

DOING BUSINESS
IN JAPAN

"Labor productivity … is considerably lower in Japan than in other major countries."

–Japan Almanac 2003

I initially thought of subtitling this "… and other ways of slitting your wrists." That's not necessarily true in the sense that there have been many entrepreneurs and businesses that have done well here. But I think all of them would agree that it was never easy!

CLOTHING

Understatement is the operative word here. The typical male office worker dresses in a dark suit (usually navy or gray), a white dress shirt, and a necktie most notable for its utter lack of any distinguishable design. His company pin will be attached to his lapel. The typical female office worker is seen in one of two styles: either a suit of a jacket and skirt, or the company uniform. Most companies have two uniforms for women, one for warm weather and the other for the rest of the year. Men and women who wear uniforms at work usually do not wear them to work; they change in locker rooms at their offices. They also have nametags affixed to their breast pockets.

As one might guess, it's best to dress accordingly when meeting on business. Brightly colored ties and shirts are acceptable for those who wish to project a hipper image. However, one should err on the side of caution when choosing one's wardrobe for the day. If people perceive your sartorial tastes to be frivolous, they are apt to take you less seriously.

OFFICE GREETINGS

Japan is the land of the stock phrase for every situation. In the glossary of this book there is a short list of greetings which will crop up at work every single day. Learning them, and consistently using them, can go a long way to help one slip into office life seamlessly.

BUSINESS CARDS

In Japan, you're nobody if you don't have a business card or other sort of name card. The business card is extremely important when first meeting someone else in Japan. Known as *meishi*, these are presented when first greeting another person in any situation that might be remotely business-related. When you receive another's card, cradle it in your hand and study it as if it were the Rosetta Stone. If you proceed to sit down, lay the card or cards on the table in front of you—this way you can discreetly glance at them if you've forgotten someone's name. Only after a suitable interval should you carefully place the card in your breast pocket or a card case—never your hip pocket! If in doubt, follow the cues provided by your opposing number.

Inkan

Almost as important as business cards are *inkan*, also known as *hanko*. These are small cylinders made of wood, plastic, or ivory with your name or company seal carved into one end. The carved end is first pressed into a red inkpad and then affixed to official documents. There are many such shops around, and you can have one quickly made for a couple of thousand yen. You can choose to have your name written either in *katakana* or, for the more exotically minded, out of *kanji* that phonetically represent your name.

An *inkan* is not required to open a bank account anymore; it is merely optional. However, some employers can still be very strict about having people sign in each day using only their *inkan*. You can also have your *inkan* officially registered at your ward office or city or town hall; however, it's not really necessary unless you plan to purchase property or do large business transactions.

You can buy little cases, complete with a miniature inkpad, to house your *inkan*. You may find that Japanese are quite interested in your *inkan*, as Japanese don't have seals composed of *katakana* lettering.

RESUMES

Resumés are terrifically important in Japan. Most jobs for English-speaking foreigners will only require you to submit an English resumé. If you want to get ahead of the game, however, you might want to include a Japanese resumé with your job application. The resumé form, called a *rirekisho*, is available from stationery shops anywhere in the country. There are a few key differences between an English resumé and a Japanese resumé worth noting:

- You will be expected to include a passport-sized photograph with your resumé. Go to a photo booth (often found near major train and bus stations) and get your picture taken.
- Biographical and professional information should be listed in chronological order, not in reverse chronological order like most Western resumés.

- Some categories may be surprising to you by their presence (commutation time and expenses) or absence (references).
- Above all, the Japanese resumé should be handwritten, not typed, and it should be done by you, not someone writing on your behalf. Penmanship is considered indicative of the person, so a neatly written resumé may very well make a very good impression on whomever reads it. To put it another way, if you've ever wanted to practice writing Japanese, now's your chance.

One example of Japanese dedication is that, typically, employees will first decide to quit their current jobs before looking for their next jobs. Though there are some people who will slyly set up new employment before quitting their present jobs, it is tremendously important in Japan to be seen as having thoroughly completed one's obligations to one's present boss. Only then can one have the purity of motive to start job hunting elsewhere.

SETTING UP BUSINESS IN JAPAN

Many foreigners in Japan have done well setting up restaurants or bars. The idea, for example, of having Australian cuisine (what? pies and beer?) served by a real Australian who can cook a fair bit makes for a unique dining experience in Japan.

One common piece of advice is to arrive with enough capital in your pocket to set things up. Brand-new equipment can be expensive for sure—what can be more expensive is buying secondhand equipment, then finding out the real reason why the original owner got rid of it. And while designing a restaurant interior can take a lot of money, it can take even more to redo later if you're not satisfied the first time.

A second, and related issue, is that the thing (whatever it is) that is so common in your home country and which you feel is absolutely necessary to get started is just not to be had in Japan. You may need a friend at home to help you order the things you want, and even if you do get it you may discover that people in Japan have no idea what you've got. One barkeep I know was shocked when he called the local distributors of a major soft drink company and asked whether his American-ordered soda guns would fit onto the locally distributed soda tanks. It turned out that they certainly did, but what he couldn't get over was the ignorance of the soft drink sales representatives. "They had never even *seen* a soda gun," he said incredulously. Remember too that while the Internet is a wonderful ordering tool for people living overseas, there are unscrupulous merchants who will take your money and fail to deliver. You may have more protection if you get what you want delivered to you while you are in your home country.

A third common problem is that the quality of craftsmanship you hire to build your place may appear incredibly poor compared to the standards you've come to expect at home. If you've got a certain idea in mind, you're going to have to repeatedly explain what it is you want. You will also very likely have to closely monitor the work that is being done. If it's not what you want you of course have the right to tell him what it is you want. Just don't expect to win any friends in the process!

Getting a restaurant or a bar started is surprisingly easy—no licenses are necessary, not even for serving alcohol. Practically the only requirement of the local health department is that there be a sink near the kitchen entrance where employees may wash their hands. The downside of all this laxness is that it is of course easy for everyone else to start a restaurant or bar as well, so you may find it difficult to break out against the competition.

WORKING IN A JAPANESE COMPANY

There are two things immediately apparent about how different life is in a Japanese company: wretched steel gray desks crammed together into groups and warm-up exercises in the morning. Both are annoying.

Contracts (*keiyaku*) are of course part of the Japanese business system, though in the past many people disdained them because

STACKS AND ROWS. *Offices everywhere look like this—rows of gray steel desks, piled high with papers.*

contracts seemed to reflect cold international norms rather than warm Japanese understanding. Japan seems to be slowly waking up to the fact that contracts are a key element to doing business in the rest of the world, so they are grudgingly trying to create a culture of contract law. At present, however, the result seems to be that if a company finds itself contractually disadvantaged with one of its employees, it will ask for the employee's understanding in resolving the problem. Yet if the employee finds himself at the short end of the stick, the company will frigidly insist that rules are rules. Be aware of the contract you negotiate!

If Japan's unemployment rate seems comparatively low to other countries, it's partly because many companies employ incompetent driftwood that for one reason or another can't be let go. If you manage to secure employment in a Japanese company, be advised that the more promise you show, the more work you'll be given, because there may be no one else in your department who can do much more than organize the colored pencils in his desk. Day-to-day management in a Japanese company can be appallingly bad, since managers are largely out of touch as to what goes on; the general feeling seems to be, "Well, if they're all staying late they must be working hard." As to what the employees are doing, however, the Japanese manager may have little idea. Many managers can't set priorities or deadlines.

Japanese society sees people constantly breaking off into various factions. In companies, that means perpetual turf wars between departments. Many Japanese managers who find their departments under consideration for oblivion will fight to the end — they just can't let go. To preserve face and to demonstrate the social requirement of respecting everyone's feelings, meetings will stretch on ad infinitum.

Everybody stays past official quitting time. One British friend of mine tried an experiment: He stayed until 10 p.m. and didn't do a damn thing all day. When he finally left, everyone congratulated him on his effort. The next day he worked like a dog, but walked out the door at 5:30 p.m. Everyone was wondering how he had the nerve to go home so early as he must not have worked hard. The Japanese employee is a master of doing eight hours of work — or less — in a 12-hour day.

Finally, do not expect any meaningful feedback regarding your job performance.

Managing the Japanese Worker

More often than not, the Japanese worker is one of the most put-upon workers in the world. There are many beautifully written laws to protect him, most of which remain mere decoration because the government seems to have no interest in actively checking that companies toe the line.

The most common abuse is obviously in the overtime people are expected to put in. Many contracts will state the working day as being something like 9 a.m. to 5:30 p.m. Good luck finding a company that actually adheres to those hours! Many people put in a 10-, 12-, 14-, or

16-hour workday—even six days a week. There is such a thing as overtime pay, but overtime in Japan is merely 20 percent more per hour. And most workers don't even get that. The average Japanese is reported to work on average something like four hours of overtime a week, but this is a sheer prevarication as companies flat-out lie and underreport the overtime their workers do. The smaller the company, the more likely this will happen.

The second-most common sort of abuse is the transfer. Because the Japanese are aware of their tendency to splitting into factions, companies randomly shuffle workers around from one branch to another. The argument for doing this to everyone is that it's "fair", which is true in the sense that it's fair if everyone's personal life gets trashed equally. Corporate Japan could go a long way to repairing the damage it has done to families by merely letting husbands and daddies stay with their families instead of moving them halfway across the country like *shougi* chess pieces.

Given that climate, it is no wonder then that many Japanese say they prefer working for a foreign company over working for a Japanese company. No matter how hard a foreign company works its employees, no matter how much it asks of its Japanese workers, it can never embrace them as suffocatingly as a Japanese company would. Japanese women especially may prefer working in a foreign company, as they will feel reasonably certain that sexual harassment will be less and opportunities for advancement will be greater.

Some Japanese are so conditioned to putting in unpaid overtime that you in fact may have to directly order some people to stop working during lunch, or use more of their paid leave, or go home at a reasonable hour. There are a number of large Japanese firms that have started turning off their electricity after a certain hour and locking the company doors one day each week. Not only are they trying to stop people from killing themselves, they're also trying to save on their utility bills. And beware the employee who turns up with a case of the flu so bad that he instantly infects everyone else. Even though his behavior is thoughtless, he'd still rather turn up sick than deprive everyone of his presence—and everyone else will do their best to emulate him.

The downside to employing Japanese workers, as one American employer told me, is that it can be hard to find self-directed, self-motivated employees. Many workers have spent virtually their entire lives being told what to do by their parents, teachers, and bosses. More importantly, they were often discouraged for thinking and acting independently. So when the time comes and they have to figure out what to do by themselves, many of them simply can't do it—they'd rather just turn up at work hung over every day and collect their paychecks each month. It may take a foreign employer time to sift the wheat from the chaff.

In fact, a lot of managers today tell me that it is getting harder and harder to find quality employees ready to start work right after college. It is difficult to say whether this is a fault of perception on their part ("Kids today have it easy compared to when I was starting out.") or an accurate analysis as to what the country's shrinking numbers of youth really means for Japan's future.

If you're going to be managing Japanese workers, remember that foreign managers can sometimes be downright intimidating to the Japanese, who are used to undemonstrative, restrained bosses. The non-Japanese boss who becomes loud and angry easily can be so off-putting that some Japanese workers will conspire to make sure that only good news is presented to the boss. The manager who learns to control his feelings at work will be able to work better with his employees in the long run.

Finally, remember that there are those people who simply will not volunteer information that you might think is important or interesting. Whether it is out of politeness or a desire to have some sort of edge is hard to say, but the good manager will be able to think of the questions he should be asking—and probe accordingly.

IMPORTING TO JAPAN

As you might already know, importing into Japan is a hard thing. Food and drink are notoriously difficult to bring in, as the country has many rules in place banning certain ingredients. Even for less problematic imports like chemicals or machinery, it seems that the government officials checking imports take a perverse joy in finding the smallest reason for rejecting an entire import. If one document is missing, if one packing seal has come off during shipment, customs will simply slam the door shut.

Perhaps Japan's biggest need at present is ideas. Business models and models for research and development are highly sought after, and foreign companies that have expertise in R&D and law may find a willing market in Japan. Perhaps even one day the investment field will be opened as well, though don't hold your breath.

No businessman can expect to visit unannounced and make a presentation, then go home and just wait for the phone to ring. It requires preparation; you have to lay the groundwork with companies in Japan so that they will truly want your product when you finally do arrive to show your wares. Fortunately, many countries have established offices that promote trade and investment in Japan. Contact the one in your country for information and help.

NEGOTIATING WITH THE JAPANESE

Boy Scout or no, negotiating with the Japanese means that you should be prepared. You can be confident that your opponent has thoroughly done his homework and has considered every possible angle. Maybe some of those angles exist only in the realm of the fantastic, but if it comes up he will be ready for it.

Do not expect to deal directly with top management. Some executives know what is going on; most don't. Often middle-level people will do the actual deal-making, and the senior person will approve it or reject it on his subordinates' advice.

Do not mistake the constant nodding of "yes, yes" to mean

agreement. Japanese are perpetually saying "*hai, hai*" to each other merely to show that they are paying attention and haven't fallen asleep. It does not mean, however, that they are enthusiastically endorsing your proposal. Nor should you be put off by bizarre or incomprehensible comments made by the other party. Chalk them up to an inability to speak English well.

Direct bribery would appear crass. However, anything that is conducted under the rubric of "entertainment" shows thoughtfulness and a willing to get to know one's client better. It often seems that the establishment of a close working relationship is almost more important than turning a profit. Almost.

Do remember that the two biggest problems in negotiation are usually language misunderstandings, and a lack of knowledge about relevant laws. It is strongly suggested that you reconfirm everything. Problems should be headed off before things get put into motion.

BUSINESS AND THE LAW

Although modeled after elements in European and American law, Japanese law is a different creature and should be respected as such. The major difference is that the legal system in Japan is deliberately stacked against using the courts to make any significant changes, at least in your lifetime. Lawyers are talented; they are also scarce. There are only about 20,000 lawyers in the entire country. Consequently, you are going to have to pay through the nose AND wait a long, long time before judgment is rendered. I'm not saying that it is wrong to do so, just advising you of the reality.

Given the fact that judgment at even the district court level can take years, a judge will often urge both parties to work out an equitable agreement so as to avoid going to court. If one party refuses to do so and insists on having his day in court, judges have been known to become prejudiced against that particular party.

There is, however, one ray of light in all this. Small claims court in Japan is easily accessible for claims of up to 300,000 yen. The cost of filing will be 3,000 yen at most, and though you're entitled to bring along the expensive lawyer of your choice, a Japanese-speaking friend should suffice. For more help, look at the following website: **http://homepage1.nifty.com/domonsaito/houritu.htm**.

INCOME TAXES

Income taxes are due 15 March. If you work for one company as a payroll employee, your company will file for you. If you work for many companies, you will have to do the paperwork yourself. The forms can be intimidating, but really there's not too much figuring to be done.

The amount of tax you should pay in one year depends upon your salary in the previous year. Your tax rate in your first year of employment will therefore be simply wonderful, but if your salary went down as compared to the year before, you're going to get hit with one painful bill.

TEACHING

A number of expatriates, including yours truly, have made a living or something by teaching English in Japan. Most of the work involved centers on teaching English conversation, but some courses require an additional understanding of writing, business, or science.

Japan has a large number of English conversation school chains, many of them concentrated near major train stations. There are also uncountable smaller neighborhood schools in areas where the chains do not reach, although these may be simple husband-and-wife operations that do not require any paid help. Employment is frequently available, however, at the larger English schools. The biggest chain is NOVA, but other large schools include Berlitz, Aeon, and Geos. Employment with these schools can be arranged before departure from your home country, but many times teachers can get better working conditions by negotiating with schools in Japan. A bachelor's degree is usually the minimum degree necessary to obtain employment, but if you don't have one your case is certainly not hopeless.

Universities, high schools, and the like also employ native teachers of English, though the recent trend has been away from full-time contracts and toward part-time contracts that are re-evaluated each year. Generally speaking, a bachelor's degree is the minimum to teach English at university, although increased competition in recent years means that some universities only consider candidates with master's degrees, particularly for full-time employment. A degree does not have to be in TESOL (Teachers of English to Students of Other Languages) or other similar field of study, but it certainly is a plus.

Information on employment can be found on such websites as Ohayo Sensei (**www.ohayosensei.com/**) and EFLweb (**www.eflweb.com/**).

JET Program

The JET Program had its genesis in the late 1980s as a way to bring young, native speakers of English and other languages to Japan so that they might be exposed to Japanese culture and contribute to the foreign language education of Japanese students. From its small beginnings it grew until today there are some 4,000 ALTs (Assistant Language Teachers) in the country. Most ALTs do not teach classes by themselves; instead, they are paired with Japanese teachers of English to team-teach students.

Supervised by three ministries, the system has had its ups and downs, but by and large it has done what it intended to do. Many foreigners, myself included, were grateful for the opportunity to live and work in Japan on the terms of the JET Program. The question now is whether the country's deteriorating economy can afford to sustain the lavish JET Program. Currently there is movement afoot for school boards to make an end run around the requirements of the JET

Program and instead hire foreign teachers directly and at lower cost. Whether this will lead to the ultimate demise of the JET Program is anyone's guess, but it seems likely that schools in outlying areas at least will want to continue with the program.

To find out more about the eligibility requirements of the JET Program, contact the Japanese embassy in your country, or visit the Ministry of Foreign Affairs' site at **www.mofa.go.jp/j_info/visit/jet/**

HOSTESSING (AND HOSTING)

One of the peculiarities of Japan's after-hours culture is the phenomenon known as the 'snack.' It doesn't mean a meal! Snack is short for snack bar, where businessmen pay astonishingly large amounts of money to have a beautiful young woman sit at the table with them, pour their drinks, light their cigarettes, engage them in conversation—*and that's all!* Many a woman has worked at such a place, earned a lot more cash than at her day job, and improved her Japanese speaking skill to boot. And, although much rarer, there are also similar host bars, where young men can perform the same sort of mundane activities for either adventurous or lonely-hearted housewives.

Obviously, working at an establishment that is part of the "floating world" (or "water business") carries the possibility of dangerous involvement with the underworld. A British woman was shockingly murdered, and there is more than one account of a woman who has "disappeared"—presumably kidnapped by a prostitution ring and enslaved. If you decide to become a hostess, do so with your eyes open and be aware of the dangers. A reference from another foreigner that you personally trust is usually the safest recommendation.

MODELING

Japanese advertising has an oddly enduring fascination with foreign models. It's not only the top-ranked Hollywood stars who get paid big bucks to endorse forgettable products; many foreigners that to your eyes look otherwise unremarkable can earn a bit of money by posing for magazines and TV ads. There are talent agencies that specialize in foreign models, so if you're interested, check out the advertisements of your local English magazine. All nationalities can usually find some modeling work depending on the product, but children, especially blond-haired children, are particularly sought after.

VOICEOVERS

Radio stations, subway trains, and airports all need or want announcements spoken by native speakers of English. Most jobs are found simply by being in the right place at the right time, usually because someone likes the sound of your voice. The work is usually a one-off opportunity, but it can pay handsomely.

"CLERGYMEN"

Another growing occupation is that of the marrying "clergyman". A popular option for Japanese couples these days is to be married, not at a traditional Shinto shrine, but at the chapel attached to a hotel or wedding hall. These pseudo-Christian venues come complete with a foreigner clothed in impressive raiment and ready to lead the man and woman in their wedding vows. Ninety-nine percent of the time the foreigner isn't a licensed minister, but then maybe that's OK because a wedding service in Japan has absolutely no connection to the legality of a couple's marriage. Foreigners who are dressed and perform as religious leaders are merely considered part of the scenery in a show. Employment requires extensive connections and introductions, but once established, it can be quite lucrative indeed.

UNIONS

Some foreigners who have lost their jobs will resign themselves to their fate, saying that the deck is stacked against non-Japanese. It's not necessary to do so because it's not true. There is at least one Japanese

133

union which is open to foreign workers, whether they are teachers or other professionals. The National Union of General Workers provides counseling and assistance for its members, and works to protect and enhance its members' rights. It is based in Tokyo, but it has branches throughout the country. For more information, visit **http://nambu.generalunion.org/** or call (03) 3434-0669 and fax (03) 3433-0334.

Chapter Eight

TELECOMMUNICATIONS

"In comparing government statistics and private statistics on Internet population, a difference of more than 10 million people is found ... and the government's statistics are consistently higher."

–Japan Almanac 2003

As in so many other ways, Japan is a mix of cutting-edge technology and old-fashioned, burdensome rules. This is apparent, for example, in the telecommunications industry.

PHONES

Home phone service is provided by Japan's giant utility NTT. Getting a home phone is a rather expensive proposition in the beginning. That is because one needs to apply for a telephone line on a subscription basis, which at present costs 76,000 yen. You may be able to purchase the right to a telephone line from an individual for much less than that, however; check the classified ads in your local English-language magazine or on your community bulletin board. If you choose to rent a telephone line, the cost is 2,390 yen for an analog line and 3,470 yen for an ISDN line. You will need to provide sufficient ID, and you will have to purchase the telephone and/or fax machine yourself at an electronics store.

Of course, make sure you tell your friends abroad to drop the first zero of the area code before dialing your home telephone number. I must have neglected this point, which is why nobody calls, I'm sure.

For more information, check out the website maintained by NTT West at **www.ntt-west.co.jp/index_e2.html** or call (0120) 36-4463. The English-speaking staff will arrange a three-way conversation between you and your local NTT representative.

Cellular Phones

One of the biggest trends in recent years is that *everybody* carries a cell phone these days. Called *keitai* (literally, "portable"), cell phones and service are provided by three major domestic companies (Docomo, Vodafone, and au) and international firms such as Nokia. There are also variations of cell phones called PHS, which are cheaper but are rapidly disappearing as more powerful cell phones continue to proliferate. Japanese cell phones are generally smaller than the typical Western phone, but probably have more bells and whistles on them than you've seen at home.

Setting up a cell phone account is probably easier than getting home phone service squared away. Cell phone shops are everywhere; find one you like and choose a phone. The latest models may be a tad expensive, but there are equally good phones priced at 100 yen or less (no kidding!) You will need to provide satisfactory ID and choose what kind of services you want. The staff may not be able to speak English well, so if you're concerned take a friend.

Cell phones have changed the way people think about style. For one, watch sales have gone down, as people now consult their phones for the time. For another, the phones are available in a variety of colors and styles, and are often decorated with some sort of attachment—or in the case of the typical high-school girl's phone, a multitude of beads, flashing lights, and animated cartoon characters. It seems that no one is immune to infantilization. While waiting on the train platform, I saw a very handsome young man, attired in a crisp black suit, reach into his jacket and pull out his cell phone—which boasted a pink Hello Kitty hand strap. All his previous coolness suddenly, and laughably, evaporated.

TRADITION AND CONTEMPORARY TRENDS. *A kimono-clad young woman using a cell phone.*

The omnipresence of cell phones has prompted all sorts of "manner-up" campaigns, which have met with fair results. The aforementioned high school girl screams into her phone much less now than she did some years ago. Movie theaters and trains constantly encourage people not to use their phones while seated, and some JR trains now have designated cell-phone areas where people can speak on their phones in relative privacy. Most of the returning calm, however, is probably due not so much to people's better manners but rather the advent of e-mail messaging, which allows people to type out their thoughts with their thumbs. It is a common sight to see a large mass of people enter the train and sit down, then promptly whip out their cell phones and begin typing away, their eyes intent on their miniature screens. Sometimes it (scarily) feels like George Orwell's Big Brother has gotten hip and awarded everyone a stylish, personal video screen.

Pay Phones

Calling from a pay phone to anywhere in the country is very easy to do. There are three sorts of pay phones in Japan: gray, green, and the rapidly disappearing pink phones. Pink phones, usually located in small eateries and pubs, are coin-operated phones. Gray and green phones accept coins (no change given) or telephone cards. Gray phones will have ISDN sockets, just in case you've got to plug your computer in somewhere.

With the widespread acceptance of cellular phones, not only are pay phones disappearing but also telephone cards are sadly less prevalent than they used to be—one of my favorite shops used to be a store that sold nothing but phone cards, all with an incredible variety of designs. However, phone cards can still be had for purchase from inside pay phone booths, at convenience stores, and at selected souvenir stands. There are two kinds of cards: the 500-yen card is available for 500 yen, and the 1050-yen card is priced at 1,000 yen. Local calls are priced according to the length of the call, just like long-distance calls.

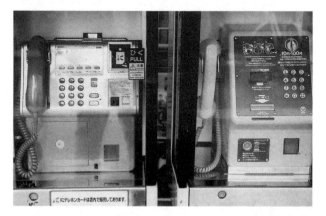

YOU RANG? *On the left is an IC card telephone for international calls, on the right a regular green, or more recently, gray, phone for domestic calls.*

For a local call, dial only the number. For a long-distance call within the country, preface the number with the area code; thus dialing Osaka from Tokyo requires (06) before the number.

If you've used up all the money in your telephone card, you can place it in a recycling box, but a thoughtful option is to just leave it lying somewhere in the phone booth. Some people make a hobby out of collecting the cards and will peek inside a booth to see if anyone's left a card behind.

International Calls

International calls can be made from orange IC phones using IC cards, which can be purchased from a vending machine directly under the phone. You can also use regular gray or green domestic phones, provided you purchase a special international calling card available at major convenience stores. Some stores sell actual cards, while others require you to navigate an in-store touchscreen computer—take the printout and your money to the counter and you will receive a second piece of paper complete with dialing information. To make an international call, follow the steps written in various languages that are posted above the phone or on the calling card.

Currently there are four providers of long-distance service: KDDI (001), NTT Communications (0033), Japan Telecom (0041), and IDC (0061). To make your call, first dial the number of the provider you choose, then 010, then the country code, and finally the area code (dropping that first "0") and telephone number itself.

Some companies offer rechargeable phone cards that can be used for international calls from cellular phones. One such company is Brastel; for more information, visit **www.brastel.com**.

Telephone Hints and Tips

Remember that area codes in Japan change progressively across the nation from northeast to southwest; thus Hokkaido is (011) and Okinawa is (098). Most toll-free numbers begin with the prefix

(0120). Cellular phones begin with either (090) or (080) and PHS numbers begin with (070); a call to any of these is more expensive from a regular phone than from another cell phone or PHS. Also, phone companies do not provide itemized billing unless specifically requested when you set up service.

One recent scam to beware of is the "*wan-giri*", the trick by which your cell phone will ring just once, leaving the caller's unfamiliar number in your phone's memory. So you, thinking it must be a friend of yours, will return the call—only to find it is really the number of a telephone sex service or some such. Even if you hang up right away, it is very likely that you will be charged for initiating the call, which means it will appear on your bill at the end of the month. Good luck arguing with the phone company about your 50,000-yen bill! My advice? If it's an unfamiliar number, go to a pay phone and pop in a 10-yen coin to make a call and identify the caller's identity first.

INTERNET ACCESS

Internet access is available at Internet cafés, as well as print shops such as Kinko's. A Japanese Internet café, however, has services far and beyond what you'd probably find at home. Beyond the simple matter of computer access, good cafés will also offer private lounges with cable TV, video and DVD players, and video games. You can get free soft drinks, and beer and food can be delivered to your lounge. If you want something to read, there will also be a selection of magazines and an astonishing collection of comic books. These places have memberships and fees that are competitively priced and worth checking out.

Internet Providers

There are many Internet providers in Japan, including America OnLine. Internet service via cable television is provided by J-COM, while Yahoo!BB and Fusion GOL offer dial-up services. Fusion GOL is also helpful with its native English-speaker support. Take a look at the following websites for more information:

- Fusion GOL: **http://home.gol.com/index_e.html**
- Yahoo!BB: **http://bbpromo.yahoo.co.jp/**
- J-COM: **http://www.jp.home.com/**
- America OnLine: **http://www.jp.aol.com/**

Remember that in Japan local calls, not just long-distance ones, are charged per minute. If you choose dial-up service, you may find yourself hit with hefty charges if you do a lot of Internet surfing.

In addition to providing either dial-up or ADSL Internet service, you can also set up your telephone to use the Internet to make phone calls. Both international and domestic calls will be cheaper, and if you call a friend who has the same service, your call should be free.

–Chapter Nine–

EATING IN JAPAN

"Raisins stuffed with dough, and then baked."
–From a box of raisin cookies seen in Japan

Sushi is one of the few foods in Japan with which it is permissible—indeed, *de rigueur*—to eat with your hands. I found this out when, not long after arriving in Japan and being extremely proud of my newfound ability with chopsticks, I started eating my *sushi* with them. The white-hatted *sushi* chef impassively stared at me, then calmly reached over the counter and took the chopsticks away from me. I looked at all the other diners who were picking up *sushi* in their right hands and got the idea. Well, if you insist …

The Japanese don't eat as much raw fish as Americans eat hamburgers and hot dogs. There is a lot of variety in dining, particularly in the cities, and there are lots of Japanese who are more familiar with eating their noodles with Italian tomato sauce than Japanese fish broth. Still, you can't live in Japan without going out for Japanese food eventually, and I know many newcomers to Japan who have gotten over their initial dislike of the food and embraced it whole-heartedly. Like me.

MEATS AND FISH

- *Sushi*–Traditional form is known as *nigiri-zushi*. *Inari-zushi* is a rice ball wrapped in sweetened tofu skin. *Chirashi-zushi* is vinegared rice served in a bowl and topped with strips of fried eggs, pickles, toasted seawee, and other toppings.
- *Sashimi*–Raw fish slices. *Sushi* without the rice.
- *Temakizushi*–Rolled *sushi*. Comes pre-rolled or you can roll it yourself.
- *Basashi*–Raw horse meat. Allegedly good. Can't be any worse than the raw deer I once ate.
- *Fugu*–Blowfish roulette. If it's prepared incorrectly you die almost instantly. And no, it's not funny to feign death and drop your chopsticks.
- *Kujira*–Whale meat. Served at more expensive parties. A sure-fire conversation starter.
- *Sakana furai*–Fried fish.
- *Yakizakana*–Grilled or broiled fish.
- *Tempura*–Nearly always includes batter-dipped and lightly fried shrimp. Other ingredients include mackerel, green pepper, mushrooms, sweet potato, eggplant, and mushroom.
- *Kakifurai*–Fried oysters.
- *Takoyaki*–Fried, doughy octopus balls. A common snack found at roadside stands or at little trucks parked near train stations at night.
- *Teppan'yaki*–Steak cooked Japanese style.
- *Tonkatsu*–Breaded and fried pork cutlets. Served at restaurants where you can often get free refills of rice, soup, cabbage, and pickles.

- *Chikin katsu*–The chicken version of the previous.
- *Yakitori*–Japanese shish kebab. Chicken, sausages, green pepper, garlic, squid, and even whole (de-feathered) sparrows are available.
- *Kara'age*–Boneless fried chicken.

NOODLES

- *Udon*–Flour noodles served in a hot broth. Sometimes served with *tempura*.
- *Soba*–Buckwheat noodles served in a hot broth. *Soba* washed in cold water and dipped in a dark soup before eating is *zarusoba*; when served with a sticky white potato sauce it is called *tororosoba*.
- *Raamen*–Japanese version of the Chinese *la mian*. Seemingly found within 100 meters of every pachinko parlor. Thin wheat noodles in a pork broth served with roast pork, bean sprouts, garlic, and sesame seeds. As one of my *raamen*-devotee friends has pointed out, the worse the smell from the *raamen* shop, the better the *ramen*. If you still have some broth left over, you can order a refill of noodles called *kaedama*.
- *Hiyashi-chuuka*–Ramen noodles served cold in a spicy gravy and topped with strips of fried eggs, ham, cucumbers, and pickles.
- *Champon*–Nagasaki's noodle dish with pork, cabbage, and fish sausage in pork broth.
- *Saraudon*–Thick *champon* poured over dried Chinese noodles.
- *Soumen*–Noodles drawn from ice water and dipped in a special broth, served with sliced cucumber, egg, ham, and miniature oranges. Popular in summer.
- *Yakisoba*–fried noodles with ham, cabbage, and carrots.

RICE

- *Teishoku*–Not a particular food as such, just the name for a set meal. Usually includes rice, soup, pickles, and a main dish.

- *Bentou*–The boxed lunch of Japan. Can come with anything.
- *Mochi*–Incredibly chewy rice cakes. Some older people actually choke to death on them.
- *Karee raisu*–Mildly spicy Japanese curry and rice, sometimes served with beef, fried chicken, or pork cutlets.
- *Yakimeshi*–Fried rice. Also known by its Chinese name of *chaahan*.
- *Dorai karee*–Fried rice mixed with curry paste.
- *Onigiri*–Rice balls. They come plain or with some kind of filling.
- *Omuraisu*–Rice omelets.
- *Domburi*–A bowl of rice with a topping. *Gyuudon* is rice topped with thinly-sliced beef, *katsudon* is topped with egg and a fried pork cutlet, *chikin katsudon* is rice topped with a fried chicken cutlet, *tendon* is rice topped with egg and shrimp tempura, and *oyakodon* is topped with pieces of chicken fried together with eggs and leek.

VEGETABLES
- *Toufu*–Bean curd. You already knew that.
- *Nattou*–Fermented soybeans. The litmus test as to whether you can fit into Japan. However, more foreigners like *nattou* than Japanese like Vegemite.
- *Daikon*–White radishes, often grated as a topping.
- *Umeboshi*–Pickled plums that adorn bowls of white rice like the Japanese flag.
- *Nori*–Dried seaweed.

SOUPS
- *Miso* soup–Red or white soybean paste soup. Usually served with *toufu*, seaweed, green onions, and mushrooms. Delicious but high in sodium.
- *Suimono* soup–Clear soup with seaweed and sesame seeds.

SHARED COURSES

- *Yaki'niku*–Barbecued beef, shrimp, onions, carrots, green peppers, and some unrecognizable cow parts.
- *Sukiyaki*–Japanese hotpot: beef and vegetables boiled in a sweet, dark broth and served with raw egg.
- *Nabe*–Covers a variety of hotpot dishes boiled in kimchee, *miso*, or other flavors. *Motsu-nabe* is full of those same unrecognizable cow parts.
- *Shabu shabu*–Hotpot with thinly-sliced pork or beef gently boiled and dipped in peanut sauce.

OTHER FOODS

- *Oden*–Boiled sausages and vegetables. Popular in wintertime.
- *Okonomiyaki*–Japanese pancakes. Not for breakfast!
- *Gyouza*–Steamed or fried Chinese dumplings. Often served with *raamen*.

CONDIMENTS

- *Shouyu*–Soy sauce.
- *Soosu*–Worcester sauce.
- *Wasabi*–Sinus-clearing horseradish.
- *Shouga*–Ginger. Slices of it cleanse the palate in between bites of sushi.
- *Furikake*–Rice seasoning.
- *Tsukemono*–Pickled vegetables.

CHOPSTICKS

If you are as terrified as I was about using chopsticks and think that you will just waste away into oblivion because you can't even feed yourself, fear not! Chopsticks are not all that difficult to use. As you can see from your fellow diners, the chopsticks should act as an extension of your index and middle fingers. Two things you should

remember: 1) Keep the tips even with each other. 2) Don't focus on snagging the food–focus instead on bringing the tips together. If you can do that, you will discover that the food has magically nestled between your chopsticks.

I suppose I should make a small mention here about Japan's wasteful chopstick use. Restaurant diners are usually presented with wooden chopsticks (*waribashi*) which are pulled apart, used once, and then thrown away. How many trees have been sacrificed in this way is beyond count. If you feel sufficiently motivated, you can do as I do and get yourself a set of reusable chopsticks, complete with a little carrying case. My set was a present; it came in a lovely wooden box just stuffed with wood shavings used as packing material and wrapped in heavy paper. It took a lot of dining out just to make up for the packaging.

OTHER RESTAURANTS

There's not only Japanese food to be had. Other foreign food is in abundance, too, though you may find new twists on what you thought you'd ordered. At the hotel breakfast buffet, mixed in with the scrambled eggs and sausages, you will likely find French fries and green salad. Convenience stores sell spaghetti sandwiches. And pizza was apparently destined to be wholly reinvented by avant-garde chefs. Forget the pepperoni—how about mayonnaise, tuna, and broccoli? Toss on the unidentifiable seafood bits! Take away that tomato sauce base—let's replace it with curry paste! And pour on the corn!

Ordering at restaurants is easy even for the uninitiated. Many restaurants have plastic food displays outside that are assiduously studied even by the Japanese themselves. It's easy to get too carried away by this; I caught myself choosing one restaurant's pork cutlet with egg on rice over another restaurant's, solely because the first restaurant's plastic food display was newer and better-looking!

You will usually be given a hot or cold towel (*oshibori*) upon sitting down. It is for wiping your hands before dining; men can also get away with wiping their faces. Some restaurants will also have a menu with Romanized letterings for dishes, or perhaps even a picture menu. The latter can be particularly useful, as I found when my salad arrived without asparagus. "But the picture on the menu shows asparagus," I protested, and what could the restaurant do but add it?

Since there is no tipping, the waiter will virtually never return to your table to find out how your meal is (or, for that matter, tell you his name). You will have to flag him down if you want something later, particularly if you need a refill of your oh-so-tiny water glass. Some restaurants, in order to spare their customers the embarrassment of having to wave their arms like they are launching an auto race, will have a plastic buzzer on the table. Push the button and the waiter will usually come sprinting. Also, when you've finished your meal, you will have to take the check yourself to the register and pay.

One popular option at some restaurants is the all-you-can-eat special, or *tabehoudai*. The food may either be brought to your table by the waiter, or it will be available as a buffet. There is usually a two-hour time limit. Often you will find this food special joined with an all-you-can-drink special (*nomihoudai*), at which you can consume as much alcohol in the allotted time as possible. This is a common feature, for example, at Japan's beer gardens, which are open for evening business in the summertime on department store roofs.

Some restaurant hints: In cities such as Tokyo and Osaka, the best restaurants can be fiendishly busy and you will find yourself standing in line for dinner, particularly on the weekends. Conversely, many restaurants will have a two-hour table policy; after you've eaten and drunk for two hours, you should pay your bill and leave no matter

Fried chicken and Christmas cake are the most popular foods for Christmas.

how much more you want to eat or drink. Note that some pricier establishments do have a service charge that is automatically added to your bill. Exactly how much of this goes to the staff is of course undocumented.

Finally, be aware that there are a few restaurants in the bigger cities with signs in their windows announcing "No Foreigners" or something equivalent. Most of the civilized world was able to do away with discriminatory practices in public places in the 20th century, but here is Japan in the 21st century, still determined to hold the line. The official word is that it would be "difficult" for the government to forcibly make businesses give up their prejudicial ways. Regardless, what every non-Japanese knows is that, no matter how classy and tasteful the restaurant may appear, the owners are still nothing but rednecks.

FAST FOOD

If you find yourself longing for something familiar, there is of course nothing more familiar for more people than McDonald's. The three Western fast food chains which will be found in abundance throughout Japan are McDonald's, Kentucky Fried Chicken, and Mister Donut. There are also domestic fast food chains; one such chain is Lotteria, which is notable for demonstrating that mediocre food is not just the province of Western corporations. An important exception is Mos Burger, which uses quality ingredients to make good, albeit small, burgers to order.

When ordering at a fast food restaurant, you should first state whether you will be taking out (*mochi kaeri*) or eating in (*koko de*). Most restaurants will have picture menus on the counter to help you get sorted out. Many restaurants sell meals as a set; if you don't want the set but only the individual item, say the name of the food and then *tampin* (single item).

DELIVERY AND TAKEOUT

Recently there has been an increase in both prepared and delivered food. Department stores will have large selections of delicious prepared food so that the wife who has been shopping all day can tell her husband, "Look what I made for you today!" You can also purchase cold foods for takeout; you will be asked how many minutes it will take you to get home so that they can pack the appropriate amount of dry ice.

Depending on the locality, you can order pizza, sushi, Chinese food, and even family restaurant dishes and have them delivered to your door. The first time you order you will have to give them your name and address, but after that you just need to say your telephone number and they will pull up your information from their computer. Most pizza menus show pictures of the shop's specials, but it is of course possible to get your own "*order pizza*".

Chinese food is often delivered on dishes, rather than in little paper boxes. Once you've finished your meal, be considerate enough to rinse them before placing them outside your door for the shop to collect the following day.

MEAL MANNERS

Japanese wait until everyone is seated and ready for the meal before saying the same Buddhist blessing (*"Itadakimasu!"*) together to begin the meal. As you eat, you may find that to your eyes there is a lot of reaching across the table for dishes; people rarely ask others to pass something to them. Also, many people seem able to eat a lot of food before needing a drink

There's no rule as to the order of courses. You will notice, however, that most people begin with soup. They stir the soup with their chopsticks—to moisten them if anything else—and drink a mouthful, then follow that with some rice. After that, they eat as they like.

Some tips on dining: When eating soup, go ahead and make as many slurping noises as you like—it's not bad manners at all. When reaching for food from a communal plate, temporarily reverse your chopsticks so that you take the food with the clean ends, rather than the ends that you have been putting in your mouth. And never, *ever* stick your chopsticks into your rice! Such a display is exactly the same as that used at Buddhist funerals, and is considered extremely ill-omened at the dinner table.

Just as people begin eating together, so too will they try to finish together—try not to be the last one left eating. When everyone is finished, people will then give thanks together for the meal (*"Gochisou-sama-deshita!"*) An unfortunate aspect of Japanese dining for Westerners with a sweet tooth is that there really is no tradition of dessert following a meal. My friend warned me that there was no hot fudge sundae forthcoming after dinner. "Japanese hot fudge sundae," he said, pointing at the pickles on my tray. Somehow, it just wasn't the same.

151

Vegetarians may find daily dining a struggle. My friend's "vegetarian" salad arrived with bacon bits and his "vegetarian" soup was made of fish broth. This can be all a bit ironic considering Japan's not-so-long-ago strict Buddhist dietary regimen, but it can be a real headache trying to explain the exact meaning of "vegetarian." There are, however, some restaurants that serve traditional Buddhist meals, known as *shoujin ryouri*, but it will take a little hunting around to find one, and these restaurants tend to be a bit expensive.

NON-ALCOHOLIC DRINKS

Because of the unbelievable proliferation of vending machines, soft drinks are available everywhere. And I do mean everywhere. You can be driving down a very country road and come upon a fork in the road that is as deserted as an Old West town just before the big shootout — yet brightly lit and standing guard at the intersection is a peppy vending machine, just ready to dispense your favorite beverage. And if you're lucky (?), it might even play a little song for you as you feed money into it.

The cola giants are well-represented in Japan, but Japan has a number of domestically produced drinks. Some of them have names presumably invented by English-challenged businessmen; one standard sports drink is known as Pocari Sweat. My personal favorites are the yogurt-flavored drinks; two popular varieties go under the unfortunately disturbing names of Calpis Water and Calpis Soda. Ignore the names and enjoy the drinks.

By contrast, fruit juices are not as popular here as they might be in your home country. They will likely be available wherever you go, but if they are they will almost certainly be plain orange, apple, or grapefruit juice.

Tea

Of course, Japan just wouldn't be Japan without its green tea. Called *o-cha*, it is served in beautiful porcelain or earthenware cups, either with a meal or by itself. Be warned, though, as traditional teacups do not have handles—if you put your fingers around the body of the cup, you will instantly discover that it is just as boiling hot on the outside as it is on the inside! Instead, use your thumb and index finger to lift the cup by the lip until the tea has cooled down a bit.

There are other varieties of tea such as *mugicha*, a caffeine-free tea made from barley, and *koucha*, which is the usual black tea. My favorite tea, however, is *matcha*. A powdered form of *o-cha*, it is the tea that is commonly served at the historic buildings and sites that tourists frequent. A typical teahouse will welcome you and ask you to choose a cup you like from amongst its collection. Then you will be shown to a *tatami* room, where you can kneel and view an exquisitely sculpted garden through an open wall. After a suitable interval, the frothy tea will be brought to you together with a small sweet. Custom dictates that you entirely consume the sweet first, then take the cup in both hands and drink the tea in three sips.

I have found the whole experience to be wonderful. As the atmosphere was right, with no other guests around and a soft wind blowing the late-morning mist through the garden, I became dreamily peaceful, with my mind becoming open to all sorts of passing thoughts. *I've left my car lights on*, I reflected, and hurriedly excused myself.

Coffee

Far more plentiful than teahouses are coffee shops. There are three basic types: the giant American chains such as Starbuck's, Seattle's Best Coffee, or Japan-based Dotour; the hole-in-the-wall sort of coffee shop adjacent to a train station and frequented by chain-smoking *sarariimen* on a break; and the little shop run apparently as a hobby, usually by an older woman. The last is the most delightful by far. It seems questionable whether all of them even turn a profit; the owner seems happy merely to serve coffee in one of a hundred different coffee cups she's acquired over the years and talk with her regular customers. The décor can be anything from "interestingly quirky" to "so uniquely bad it's almost good." Most of the shops will serve some basic dishes such as curry and rice, but a few are coffee-only. Regardless, they are veritable oases. Japan can be a noisy country, and the quiet coffee shop off the busy thoroughfare becomes a welcome refuge, if only for an hour.

ALCOHOLIC DRINKS

Beer

When people ask me to explain the *real* reason I've stayed here all these years, I shrug, scratch my head, and say, "Beer." There's

something to be said for a country that still permits beer vending machines on street corners. Although they are slated for eventual removal, it has always been a reassuring feeling to walk home, no matter how bad the day, and stroll past the white fluorescent glow of a machine that dispenses two-liter cans of lager. What, me worry?

Beer is of uniformly high quality over here. The major breweries (Kirin, Asahi, Sapporo, Suntory, Yebisu, and Orion—the latter found mostly in Okinawa) produce regular versions of good-to-excellent beers, and some of them also produce seasonal varieties. The major drawback to Japanese

COLD RELIEF. *Although slated for eventual removal, beer vending machines can still be found throughout the country.*

beer is that it can produce some rip-roaring hangovers the next day (trust me on this one). The reason for this is that most breweries will add cornstarch to their beers, which speeds the fermentation process and guarantees that the next batch of beer can be started that much faster. Yebisu is one beer that is made without cornstarch.

In recent years, Japan's ever-faltering economy has meant that the days of paying 1,400 yen for a beer in some swanky bar are disappearing (although not quickly enough, I might add.) Instead, what has taken their place is a proliferation of "100-yen beer nights." These are to be taken with a word of caution. Sometimes they serve beer, but more often it's only *happoshu*, an inferior grade of beer that on a good night is an acceptable beer substitute, and on bad nights tastes like swill. Drink with caution!

Wine and Other Spirits

Of course, there's not only beer to be had. Japan imports vast quantities of spirits from other countries. Then there are the domestically produced spirits, most of them produced by the giant distillery Suntory. I've drunk a lot of fine whiskies in my time, and I can honestly say that Suntory isn't one of them. But it is omnipresent in drinking establishments everywhere, usually served as a tasteless whiskey and water called *mizuwari*. Usually this is imbibed at the second party — and believe me, if you were invited to the first party, you'll get invited to the second as well. It is usually possible to beg off from the whiskey and water and ask for something else instead. Just be aware that the whiskey probably came from your host's "*bottle keep*", and as such was already paid for, whereas any other drink you order will just add to his bill.

Wine is also commonly available. Domestically produced wines are usually inferior. Imported wines abound, and are sometimes priced without any regard to their true value; we've found good wines at good prices and so-so wines at stiff prices. One particular wine that is very popular is the Beaujolais Nouveau that is flown in from France every November. It will be overly priced when it first arrives, but you might be able to find it later at a better price once the novelty wears off—and, apart from being "unfashionable", there's nothing wrong with a Beaujolais Nouveau after the November craze dies away.

One of the odd points of Japan is that, as often as not, you will find in a bar that the white wine is kept on the shelf, and the red wine stored in the refrigerator. While there are certainly some wines for which this would be acceptable practice, in general it seems that many bars have gotten things backwards.

Sake

Of course Japan would not be Japan without its legendary *sake*. Pronounced "sa-kay", it can be served cold or hot. Either is fine, with the hot variety seemingly entering your bloodstream that much faster. The little cups of *sake* do not have to be drained in one go like a shot glass; it is permissible to sip from them as you like. *Sake* is usually served from ceramic bottles called *isshou*.

Sake today seems to have a reputation as being a slightly effete alcohol. Rivaling *sake* in popularity, and perhaps surpassing it, is *shouchuu*. Similar to a low-grade vodka, it has overcome its formerly lower-class association and become a trendy drink of sorts. Whereas previously it was drunk mostly by middle-aged men, who would mix it with hot water, *shouchuu* is now served in cocktails. *Chuu-hai* (*shouchuu* mixed with some variety of fruit flavoring) is a popular drink, especially for women.

Obviously, drinking is a large part of the culture, allowing people to escape the pressures of their jobs. Conversely, some people find the cumulative effect of too many parties to be very unenjoyable and exhausting. Particularly demanding is the year-end party (*bonenkai*) season of November and December. Each organization, whether business, school, martial arts class, or even group of friends, will try to organize a little party to mark the passing of the year—and if you have to pay for all of them, the bill can quickly add up. You may

OH, FOR GOODNESS, SAKE. *Drums of sake, given by local corporations as religious offerings, are piled outside a shrine*

find yourself having to pick and choose from the invitations offered to you, and politely declining the rest.

Finally, one last piece of advice: If you're in a taxi going home, and you feel after too much drinking that you're ready to heave in the taxi, don't! The going surcharge is at least 10,000 yen, and usually 20,000, to clean up after you. If you feel that you just can't make it home, wait until the driver stops at a red light and ask him to open the door. (*"Doa o akete kudasai."*) He'll open the automatic door and you can lean out the side and take care of business. When you feel better, he'll close the door and continue to your home, and not a thing will be said.

–Chapter Ten–

ENTERTAINMENT

"Television is a medium of entertainment which permits
millions of people to listen to the same joke at the same
time, and yet remain lonesome."

–T.S. Eliot

Whatever your job, just make sure you save some energy for after
hours—there are a lot of things going on! No matter how you like to
fill your idle time, with a little poking around you can find something
you like doing.

NEWSPAPERS

There are four major English-language newspapers: the *Japan Times*,
Daily Yomiuri, *Mainichi*, and the *International Herald Tribune*, the

latter published in conjunction with the *Asahi Evening News*. English newspapers can be found at bookstores, hotels, and kiosks at major train stations. They can also be received by subscription. Newspaper companies will have press holidays from time to time during the year, so don't be worried if your newspaper doesn't turn up on Monday. For more information regarding newspapers, check out the following websites:

- *Japan Times*: **www.japantimes.co.jp/**
- Daily Yomiuri: **www.yomiuri.co.jp/**
- Mainichi: **http://mdn.mainichi.co.jp/**
- Asahi Evening News: **www.asahi.com/english/english.html**

MAGAZINES

The major U.S. newsmagazines *Time* and *Newsweek* can be found at kiosks located near major train stations. These will be published simultaneously in English and Japanese; make sure you get the one you want! A much greater selection of magazines in English and other languages can be found in the English section of major bookstores.

Major cities will also have at least one locally written and published English-language magazine. It will likely be heavy on ads and information about restaurants and entertainment. Some magazines may also explain aspects of Japanese culture, or examine issues affecting foreigners in Japan. One good, free publication is *Japanzine*, available in larger bookstores. Other good magazines include *Tokyo Journal*, *Kansai Time Out*, and *Fukuoka Now*.

BOOKSTORES

Most bookshops will have very little in the way of non-Japanese books. (Now go figure!) However, in most medium-sized cities there will be at least one branch of Maruzen, Kinokuniya, or Junkudou with a fair selection of English books, and perhaps some books in French and German as well. These sections will be heavy on books about Japan, country guidebooks, classic literature, English textbooks, children's books, pulp novels, and college texts. Larger cities will have more varied bookstores, of course. For hard-to-find books, Internet companies such as Amazon are still the best option.

TELEVISION

As in any other country, television provides several windows onto Japanese society: what they do, what they like, and how they wish to see themselves. In Japan's case, the viewer will undoubtedly be treated to a view of Japanese people that he never could have discerned merely by attending a lifetime of business meetings.

Like Britain with its much-vaunted BBC, Japan has its own national network, NHK. Though sometimes belittled by a few Japanese who expect it to equal or surpass the Beeb in quality, the programming on NHK can be quite good. It has by far the best news shows as well as the most frequent updates, and though some might find the programs a bit dry and stuffy, it is certainly preferable to some of the overly dramatized "news" on other networks.

NHK produces a lot of quality cultural programming. It has made the very respectable series *Musashi*, about one of Japan's legendary swordsmen, and also broadcasts classical music concerts and other highbrow entertainment. NHK also has a separate education channel. There are many children's shows on the educational channel, which are generally broadcast early in the morning, and then repeated later in the afternoon (trust me on that last point!) Children's shows in general seem to be less education-oriented than *Sesame Street* and focus more on songs and activities. Sometimes the children's shows seem a bit amateurish, but then that can also be part of their charm.

The most remarkable aspect of the education channel, to me anyway, is its foreign language classes. Usually at least two presenters — a Japanese and a native speaker of the particular language — will conduct a short, weekly program teaching people how to speak another language. Of course English is the most popular language, with not only the most broadcasts but also with the largest number of proficiency levels. But in addition to English, there are also lessons in French, Spanish, German, Chinese, and Korean, and for all I know Swahili, too. Though the actual audience they serve may be small, the effect that they have can be stunning. My friend, a Korean-American, was surprised to meet an old Japanese man in an intensely rural part of the country who spoke very credible Korean. He had, it turned out, learned it entirely by watching NHK's Korean lessons. I think of that, and then I remember watching the attempts at teaching a foreign language on U.S. military broadcasting in Okinawa ("When greeting people in Japan, say *konnichiwa*!") I wonder which country tries harder to educate its people about another country's culture.

Anyway, if it sounds intriguing to learn French via Japanese (!), you can go to your local bookseller to buy the latest month's edition of that language program's textbook. And if language isn't your thing, you can bone up on math or science, which also have their own programs. Funny – I haven't come across the NHK program teaching history, though.

Like the BBC, NHK receives public funding. This is paid for out of the government's budget—and by the monthly NHK tax. A collector will come to your door each month and ask for payment, which will be a couple of thousand of yen for a color TV and less for a B&W set. Some collectors are quite zealous, others less so. If you live in an apartment where your TV cannot receive NHK—it happens—you might be able to argue against paying the tax, or perhaps pay it only once. Curiously, though the law requires payment from each household with a TV, there is no penalty for nonpayment.

In addition to its broadcast channels, NHK also operates two "free" satellite channels, BS-1 and BS-2. Weekday mornings on BS-1 you can find a digest of the world's news programs, and during baseball season you can watch U.S. baseball games. There are also pay satellite channels (not run by NHK) such as WOWOW and Sky Perfect, and cable television is making inroads into Japanese cities everywhere.

There are also other broadcast networks, such as Fuji and Asahi, as well as multiple local affiliates. Some of the best programs can rival NHK's, but very often they plumb the depths of inanity.

In general, Japanese programs break down into the following categories:

- **"Wide Shows"** –These are essentially gossip shows disguised as news programs. A group of regular panelists will sit around a table and endlessly dissect the day's topic. The more they can sensationalize their topic, the more they'll yammer on *ad infinitum*. A real ratings-topper will be "analysis" of the latest shocking crime, with a few snippets of "shocking" footage shown again and again and again. It might be only the latest example of a Japanese politician being driven away by police on charges of malfeasance, but if that's all the network's got, then they'll be sure to repeat it, even down to the slow-motion version. Or it might be the latest celebrity wedding, with fawning interviewers gushing over every banal comment the couple makes.

  Generally speaking, the morning shows are worse than the afternoon shows, perhaps because of the limited chance each network gets to catch the attention of employees before they head off to their jobs. But there's very little to like about them any time of day. Be sure to note each panel's resident "intellectual", perhaps some self-satisfied university professor of chemistry who feels eminently qualified to offer his superior opinion on sociology, international relations, and the morals of today's young people. (Also be sure to note how politely and un-questioningly his half-baked opinions are accepted by the other panelists!)

- **Cooking Shows**–There's a surprising number of these, and they will be made in either a studio or on location, sampling local delicacies. One particularly favorite topic is *ekiben*, the boxed lunches that can only be found at one particular train station, usually in a rural area. And I will guarantee you that, when it's time to sample the food, each and every person will exclaim, "*Oishii!*" ("Delicious!") For years and years I have watched in vain for even one person to take a bite out of something, chew thoughtfully, and then confront the camera and say, "*Mazui!*" ("Tastes bad!")

Although primarily known for his counseling shows, as well as the Japanese version of *Who Wants To Be A Millionaire?*, the gray-haired Mino Monta is perhaps Japanese TV's *éminence grise*. If Monta says on his cooking show that a certain vegetable or herb is good for you, then you can be sure that it will be sold out of your nearby supermarket within hours. Monta exudes a comforting certainty, and his pronouncements on any subject are very influential.

- **Dramas** – How much bad acting and cheap sentimentality can you handle? If you want to know the answer to that question, subject yourself to a night of watching Japanese dramas.

  A voice of caution inside my head insists that the acting isn't "bad"; it's just "different". So I will temporize by saying that they are just plain annoying. Dramas are thoroughly unrealistic and heavily stylized. Characters don't have conversations, they recite monologues. Actors emote like no person you'd ever meet in real life. Dramatic meetings between two people take place in thoroughly empty classrooms, on completely deserted train platforms, or in restaurants with one waitress and no customers. Car chases in Tokyo occur along—reality check!—streets devoid of other cars. And if you have any doubt as to whether you're watching the latest moment of *pathos*, rest assured that the sniffly sound of strings will confirm you are so doing.

  Unlike dramas in other countries, which may go on for many seasons, Japanese dramas are made with a definite end in sight, usually after a few months. Then the cast and crew are broken up, to be reconstituted into new programs further down the road. In fact, a few months' acquaintance with Japanese TV will point out to you exactly how small the entertainment world in Japan really is. Actor Suzuki from Drama A is also Singer Suzuki on Singing Show B is also Comedian Suzuki on Comedy C. In the world of Japanese entertainment, everybody does everything, and nobody has the effrontery to point out that Suzuki can't sing or tell jokes or even act—he just looks photogenic.

One nice thing to point out is that, unlike American TV, which killed off the Western decades ago, samurai dramas can still be found, though they're hanging on by their fingernails. They're no great shakes, but it's good to know that programs celebrating Japan's past can still make inroads into commercial TV.

- **Variety Shows**–The situation comedy as known in many Western countries is virtually nonexistent in Japan. Instead, for comedy people turn to variety shows. And, as the name implies, they can vary tremendously in form and content.

Some of the variety shows, frankly, are not all that far removed from the perverse TV programs that were once more common-place—lots of girls in bikinis and lots of close-ups. One program, for example, showed a guy and a girl in swimsuits trying to push each other off a diving board, using only their rear ends. Ninety-nine percent of the time, the girl was pushed in, with the special "underwater cam" placed to catch her thrashing about. Or an even ostensibly "serious" program can quickly degenerate into something else entirely. One particular program purports to help people determine whether they're paying too much rent for their apartments. The camera crew and interviewer will visit the apartment to visit the tenant, who coincidentally is a girl, and they will take time going through her apartment, where coincidentally her underwear is hanging up drying, and …

While all that is certainly in questionable taste, to me the very worst aspect of Japanese humor, as expressed in the country's variety shows, is its abusiveness. For example, American humor, as perpetuated by Hollywood, is constantly making fun of upper class ways; all I have to imagine is a group of slobs who self-assuredly crash a high society party while a string quartet plays Vivaldi, and I've got the plot for more than a dozen Hollywood movies.

Such scenes are predictable, but they can be socially satisfying. (Unless you live in the Hamptons.) In any case, I find them preferable to Japanese standup comedy, which will likely as not feature two guys, one obviously superior to the other—and the laughs result when the superior knocks his inferior back into place. Sometimes it's done verbally and sometimes with a slap to the head, but in any case it leaves me feeling troubled about what people in Japan find humorous.

One program, for example, featured a family seated around a table, trying to have a conversation—while from overhead, pots and pans dropped on their heads. The trick was that they were supposed to pretend nothing was happening to them and just carry on with the conversation. I am sure the pots and pan were not made of steel but probably just aluminum—but even so, a dropped aluminum pot has still got to hurt when it hits your head. Western comedy makes fun of psychic pain—think of a character caught *in flagrante delicto*—while Japanese comedy tends to make fun of physical pain. At what exact point does it stop being slapstick and turn into something darker?

Comedies

That's not all there is to variety shows, of course. One of the enduring staples is the *manzai*, the slick banter between two comedians, usually male. Some duos go on for years, and one thing you'll notice is that, just like a Brooklyn accent was an advantage for any budding American comedian, so too is the accent and slang of Osaka.

Of the major comedic stars, perhaps the most famous internationally is Kitano Takeshi, popularly known as "Beat" Takeshi. Though he's known abroad as a director of powerful films, in Japan he's seen as a funny comedian who wears stupid wigs and over-the-top costumes. Many people also find him to be less funny these days, although whether it's due to his near-fatal motorcycle accident or his increased international stature is difficult to say.

The most popular domestic comedian is the slender Sanma, but for my money the funniest man working in Japanese TV is Shimura Ken. The last and probably the most talented performer to come out of the legendary comedic group known as the Drifters, Shimura Ken made me laugh even when I could barely understand Japanese. Some of the skits that he and his troupe performed remind me of the very best of the '70s U.S. television comedy *The Carol Burnett Show*—think of Shimura Ken as a Japanese Tim Conway, and you start to get the idea. At other times he will wander off and parody the repartee of a game show and I will be lost, or he too will fall into the trap of abusive humor and turn me off, but anytime I know he's on I will take the time to see what he's up to.

One further point: It seems that people in Japan especially feel the need to turn on the TV while they are at home, even though they're not interested in the programming *per se*. It seems people here need the reassurance of the background noise it provides. I have had guests in my own apartment decide it was too quiet and turn on the TV for me, and they couldn't begin to understand me when I calmly reached for the remote control and turned it off again.

RADIO

Broadly speaking, radio programming in Japan is a disappointment. This is largely due to the inability of Japanese DJs to—let's be blunt here—shut up. They will yammer on and on by themselves or with a partner in their oh-too-cute prattle, and they will trample over the intro, closing, or even the middle of a song with their commentary. Plus, the relative scarcity of broadcasters means that many stations do not have a format devoted to a certain kind of music, but instead play a little of this and a little of that. It's hard to find a station that plays one genre all day long.

U.S. radio programming, in the form of the Armed Forces Network, can be picked up at locations near U.S. military bases in Japan, and though it might be geared more for the tastes of young men far from home, it is still usually preferable to domestic programming. A better option, at least when you are not driving, is the cable radio package called *yuusen*. Many love hotels, and some apartment complexes, will have this available. This is a cable music service that offers an astonishing number of radio channels, segregated by format and without a lot of annoying talk; it's worth listening to if you tire of the listening only to the music you own.

This may only be me, but I can say that the most pleasurable time I've ever had listening to radio in Japan was during those times I caught a taxi home after midnight. In the wee hours of the morning, NHK will broadcast old American pop standards dating from just after the war. Are you ready for "Mr. Sandman" or "How Much Is That Doggie in the Window?" Many taxi drivers will listen to NHK all night long to help keep them awake, and listening to that music while half-asleep myself makes a nice trip down a memory lane I'm not even old enough to remember.

MOVIES

Foreign movies, most of them from Hollywood, are usually shown with Japanese subtitles (*jimaku*/ 字幕), so you can watch them with your Japanese friends and both of you can understand what is going on. A few movies, particularly animated ones aimed at children, will be dubbed (*fukikae*/ 吹き替え) into Japanese, so check first.

Japanese cinema's glory days seem to be long ago. The most famous and lauded Japanese director was Kurosawa Akira, the maker of *Rashoumon* and *Shichinin no Samurai*. The latter was the film upon which Hollywood's *The Magnificent Seven*, was based. Another talented director was Itami Juzou, who made *Tampopo*, *A Taxing Woman*, and *The Funeral* before his shocking suicide in 1996. Now, however, apart from a few bright spots like the likable comedy *Shall*

167

We Dance?, most Japanese films are predictable retreads like the *Tora-san* series or *Godzilla*. And because Japanese films are of course shown only in Japanese, your best chance to understand these films might be to rent or purchase them in your home country with the appropriate subtitles or dubbing.

Theaters will in all likelihood be more expensive in Japan than they are in your home country. However, the theater experience will also probably be much more enjoyable. Most audiences are quiet throughout (especially during comedies incomprehensible to Japanese theatergoers!) and the screens and seats are excellent. Women can get discounts on Ladies' Day (usually Wednesday), and the last show of the day is often discounted as well—because many people can't make the train afterward.

VIDEO AND DVD

Some video shops will be tiny affairs attached to (don't ask me why) dry cleaning shops, but the vast majority of video rental shops are wonderfully chock full of films that you'd be interested in. Some may only have the latest Hollywood blockbusters; others will have a great selection of older or more esoteric films than you might have initially expected. At this writing, videos are still predominant in rental shops, but newer releases are also available for rental on DVD.

Setting up a membership is easy and inexpensive. You'll have to show your identification and fill out a form with your name and address. The latest releases are usually available for one or two nights' rental; older films can usually be rented for seven nights. Most videos are subtitled (*jimaku*/字幕); however, some have Japanese voiceovers (*nihongo*/日本語). If you accidentally rent the wrong video, you may be able to persuade the staff to rent you the other version at no extra charge.

One of the nice features of many video shops is that they also rent music CDs. These can be cheaply rented and you can record them at home.

ANIME AND COMIC BOOKS

Japanese animation, known as *anime*, has become very popular outside Japan. For the life of me I can't understand why. All of the *anime* that I've had the patience to sit through has been stilted, computer-created, cheaply produced drivel. Warner Bros. in the 1940s was doing a better job at animation than Japanese studios today. But I guess I'm missing something.

Japanese comic books, or *manga*, are often tied in with *anime* and massively popular in their own right. Many coffee shops and restaurants keep stacks of *manga* on shelves so their single customers will have something to read while dining. There are series for children (*Doraemon*, a big-headed blue cat, for example, or *Dragonballz*) and others that appeal to … uh, shall we say a more *risqué* sensibility. Actually, some *manga* are quite intelligently done and provide good reading, but it's nevertheless a sad statement on the country as a whole when comic books are the preferred reading of the average commuter.

MUSIC

Traditional Japanese music is performed on a variety of instruments, including the *shamisen*, a three-stringed lute; the *shakuhachi*, a bamboo flute; the *koto*, a zither; and *taiko* drums. It is very unlikely, however, that you will hear this live; if you hear it at all, it will most likely be a recording played as background music during a festival or at a restaurant. Nor will music stores in Japan carry many CDs of it. You could likely do just as well searching through the world music section of your music store at home. Personally, I love a good *shakuhachi* performance and anything done by performers from Okinawa, which has a remarkable and eminently likable tradition of its own. And if you have the chance to catch a performance of *taiko*, you are very lucky as it is very athletic and terribly exciting.

The two most widely known Japanese musicians, to international audiences at least, are probably Ozawa Seiji and Sakamoto Ryuu'ichi. The names of both are probably familiar to the average Japanese, but unless the person is a fan of classical music or soundtracks respectively, he probably won't be able to identify anything specific either man has done.

Older Japanese will sing a type of song called *enka*. These are sentimental, even maudlin, songs that hearken back to a simpler Japan that many people feel has vanished. Ironically, these songs are usually not sung *a cappella* or with simple instruments, but with the use of the latest karaoke machine, including some very frightening reverb. If you walk past a pub at night and you hear someone bawling his heart out into an old folk tune, you're probably listening to *enka*; if the audience is rhythmically clapping along, it most definitely is. Most younger people, not surprisingly, avoid *enka* like the plague.

Japanese pop music, colloquially called J-Pops, encompasses a wide range of styles, including pop, rock, and hip-hop. It is very difficult to recommend this or that particular group, because groups really do go in and out of fashion; there is almost no Japanese pop equivalent of the Beatles, Rolling Stones, Beach Boys, or Eagles — some group whose music seems never to fade away. If I were to make one recommendation, it would probably be the Southern All Stars, although they seem to appeal mostly to thirty-somethings and above.

One group that has shown significant staying power through the years, however, is SMAP, a popular group of five male singers. SMAP illustrates what's wrong with Japanese pop music. Only two of the guys can sing with any particular distinction, and they don't even play their own instruments. They do some nimble dance steps and lip synch many of their performances. In short, they are a popular singing group because they are five good-looking, agreeable lads who have been aggressively packaged by their label. When not singing together in concert or on TV, they also work individually in different TV shows — it's very difficult to avoid them!

Foreign artists have made the rounds of Japan for years, partly because of the lucrative ticket prices they can charge, and partly because bands, especially older bands, never lose their following —

even bands that are no more. It's debatable as to whether the most popular foreign band is the Beatles or the Carpenters.

Some artists, like David Bowie, deserve kudos for showing an understanding and appreciation of Japan's culture and people. Others don't, however, because they've cheated their unquestioning fans — either by performing extremely truncated shows or by just walking out during the middle of a performance. And you can tell Janet Jackson and Oasis that I said so.

FESTIVALS AND HOLIDAYS

There are hundreds of festivals in Japan throughout the year. Some of the most charming are the ones that aren't heavily hyped by the local board of tourism. Randomly traveling through Japan and stumbling across one that wasn't even mentioned in your guide book is one of the tiny charms of Japan.

New Year's is probably the most important family holiday, which is quite ironic since most people seem to spend the holiday indoors watching TV. Traditionally, people will head to a shrine at midnight and offer their prayers for the next year to be a good one. Millions of people do this each year — I know because I live right around the corner from one of the most famous shrines in the country and the cars are all blocking my driveway — but every time I ask my students if they went to a shrine they all answer, "Nah — it was too cold."

Even for the indoors-bound, however, there are still some other important traditions. People send New Year's cards to each other called *nengajou*. The house should undergo its biggest annual cleaning. Common foods include soba (to be eaten before midnight), *ozoni* soup (to be eaten on New Year's Day), *mochi*, and the bountiful three-day spread of food called *osechi*. It's all fine, though the *osechi* does get a bit tiresome after the first day. I usually wind up making tacos by the third day.

Setsubun takes place in early February. This festival takes place about the same time as the beginning of the new year according to the traditional Japanese calendar. To mark the change, people will stand at their doorway and throw soybeans out the door while saying, "*Oni wa soto, fuku wa uchi!*" ("Devils out, good luck in!") Then you should pick up as many beans as your age and eat them.

Girl's Day, or *Ohinamatsuri*, also known as the Doll Festival (3 March), sees the display of dolls that represent a long-ago emperor and empress, as well as their panoplied retainers, on an

BANNER DAY. *Carp flags fly in front of homes and apartments prior to Children's Day.*

ornate platform. If you thought you had finally become immune to ridiculous prices in Japan, check out how much a set of these dolls cost. Boys' Day, sometimes referred to as Children's Day, is 5 May. Colorful carp flags called *koinobori* are flown at this time.

Late March and early April is the time for *hanami*. This is perhaps the most special time in Japan, as people will go out and have a picnic or barbecue in a park under the blossoming cherry trees. In crowded cities, people and companies can actually go into a public park and mark where they want to sit; the spots are easily identified with stakes, string, and a very junior member of the group sitting and waiting. Drinking sake is a very important part of *hanami*, and as the shadows get longer the parties get louder! Great fun.

The period from late April to early May encompasses three public holidays and is referred to as Golden Week. This "week" is almost always gorgeous: warm sunshine without any oppressive humidity. Many people, if they take a vacation at all, will take it at this time, with the result being that public transport is clogged with vacationers and air ticket prices go way up.

Not much happens during the Star Festival known as *Tanabata* on 7 July. Around that time you will see leafy bamboo cuttings decorated with bits of colored paper; inscribed on the paper are people's prayers for good fortune.

Summer means the appearance of fireworks (*hanabi*). Different municipalities will have fireworks extravaganzas on different days in July and August, which means that with a little get up and go you can check out a number of different festivals during the summer. They're quite enjoyable, and the festival atmosphere is enhanced by the number of young women dressed in colorful summer *yukata*. You will also see many stiff, round hand fans called *uchiwa*.

O-bon is the time when the spirits of the dead return to visit the living. It is also the most important holiday for which there is no official time off. Despite this, nearly everyone seems to take this time off to crowd the trains and roads and head to his hometown. Some places celebrate with firecrackers and parades; most towns are simply quiet with remembrance.

In the fall comes *Shichi-Go-San* (Seven-Five-Three), which is a holiday to commemorate special moments in the lives of children aged seven, five, and three. Around this time you will see many families taking their children to photo studios to have their pictures taken, either in traditional garb or contemporary clothes.

While very few people in Japan are Christian, Christmas is a very big holiday, although it is not a rest day, in Japan. Christmas lights and Christmas trees will go up in front of every department store, sometimes as early as October, and some shops will dress their staff in Santa outfits. What's bizarre, however, is how Christmas is seen as an equivalent of Valentine's Day; everyone wants to have a hot date with that special someone on Christmas Eve. Expensive dinners at nice restaurants, or perhaps a cruise on the bay, are usual romantic options, but there are also those who think a date in the balcony of a church for a candlelight service to be cool as well. For those who stay at home, the "traditional" foods are Kentucky Fried Chicken and Christmas cake. In some homes children may receive presents, too. But come the 26th of December, all the decorations are gone as the country prepares for New Year's.

The one downer to virtually every public festival is the presence of stands selling food, drink, and toys. The lines of yellow-bannered stalls have a dreary sameness about them. They all sell the same second-rate food, and more troubling is the suspicion that the *yakuza* control these concessions. Bring your own grub if you can.

BASEBALL

Baseball was brought to Japan by American missionaries in the 19th century and has since lodged itself permanently into the nation's consciousness. Today, the most popular professional team by far is the Yomiuri Giants, also known as the Tokyo Giants. Being a Giants fan for many isn't a deliberate choice, it's just something that is second nature, like wearing a dark suit or voting for the LDP. The Giants are endlessly promoted by the Yomiuri newspaper chain, which also conveniently owns a TV network, thus guaranteeing their players perpetual overexposure. That is, until the games go off at 9:30pm for other regularly scheduled programming. How fans can stand having broadcasts stopped before the final out is recorded is beyond me.

The Giants play in the Central League, as do their legendary rivals the Hanshin Tigers of Osaka. The winner of the Central League meets the winner of the Pacific League in the Japan Series in October. The Pacific League, the weaker of the two leagues in terms of attendance, does have at least one solidly supported franchise in the Fukuoka Daiei Hawks. Much of that support undoubtedly comes from the city's appreciation of the team's manager, Oh Sadaharu. The greatest player in Japanese baseball history, Oh, who is of Taiwanese descent, is a dignified gentleman and a living legend. He is not as telegenic as

SEVENTH-INNING STRETCH. *Balloons are released during a break in a baseball game.*

his former teammate, ex-Giants manager Nagashima Shigeo, who combined a famous home run, some good play, and a talent for malapropisms to become Japan's most beloved baseball personality. But Oh's world record of 868 home runs by itself is enough to move him to the head of the class.

The future of Japanese baseball, like sumo, is in doubt. Many of the weaker teams play in front of sparse crowds; occasionally the TV camera crews will screw up and show acres of empty seats. With top-name talent (Nomo, Ichiro, and Big and Little Matsui) heading off to the States and second-rate players from abroad rounding out the rosters in Japan, it seems likely that one day Japanese baseball will have to do something dramatic to survive, perhaps by merging with leagues in Korea and Taiwan.

While the professional version wrestles with serious problems, there is no doubt whatsoever about the continuing popularity of high school baseball. High school baseball is a semiannual rite, with a sudden-death tournament in spring (*haru no koushien*) and another, far more important tournament in August (*koushien*). Teams of boys aged 15 to 18 first play to qualify from their particular prefecture, then meet at Koushien Stadium in Osaka to work their way up the ladder of elimination until one team is left standing. Particularly in August, when many people have little to do during *o-bon* except watch TV, the tournament is hugely popular programming across the nation. Whether it's wise is another matter entirely. If my child were playing, I would be gravely concerned about the attention the nation's sporting press devotes to high school players. The pressures are just as great, say, as that faced by any adult male who ever played for New York Yankees' owner George Steinbrenner. As more than one sportswriter has observed, a season is the story of one winning team—and all the others that lost. Is it fair to nationally broadcast the inevitable mistakes that some teenaged boys are going to make?

Regardless, playing at *koushien* is perceived as a rite of manhood, a moment of youth that blooms oh-so-briefly and is then forever lost. The players themselves seem to know that; when they've played their final game in the tournament, they tearfully scoop up a piece of soil from the field as a keepsake and take one last look around. No matter what you think of the tournament or the sport itself, that last scene of tears shed over glory forever lost is very touching indeed.

SOCCER

In order to nurture its World Cup hopes, the soccer league known as the J-League was launched in the early '90s. It has had its ups and downs but seems here to stay. The sport received a tremendous boost in 2002 as Japan co-hosted the World Cup with Korea, and the national team performed far better than most impartial observers had predicted. Unlike professional baseball, which seems like army camp at times, J-League players play exuberantly and appear individualistic. There are teams sprinkled throughout Japan, so catching a soccer game should be no problem.

Chapter Eleven

COMMUNICATING WITH THE JAPANESE

"The problem of understanding is omnipresent.
Foreigners must often negotiate the meaning."
–CLAIR Japanese textbook

COMMUNICATING IN ENGLISH

Years ago Garry Trudeau, in his *Doonesbury* comic strip, showed a
radio talk show host complimenting his Japanese caller on the high
quality of his spoken English. The caller replied that it wasn't
anything special, really; after all, he WAS an elementary school
student.

Riiiiight.

If you've gotten it into your head that the Japanese can all speak
English fluently, you're definitely in for a rude awakening. Although

there are many people in the service industry who can speak English quite well, you would be forgiven if you assumed that nearly everyone would be able to speak some English, considering that nearly everyone had to study it for at least six years in school. The fact that many, many people cannot is a very obvious sign that there is something wrong with Japan's educational system.

If you are a native speaker of English remember that, if you speak English to a Japanese person, you are in effect conceding that you cannot converse with him about the same topic in Japanese. So by all means show some consideration for the effort that he makes to understand you. Be conscious in your choice of words; choose simpler words and make simpler sentences. Speak your sentences slowly and pause in the middle of your sentences; if you give people tiny moments to process the words that they hear, you stand a much better chance of being understood. Be aware that most Japanese learn American English, so you should usually go with American words (e.g., "apartment" instead of "flat"), although there are certainly exceptions. Finally, learn how to say "Do you speak English?" in Japanese; it's simple courtesy!

If you cannot communicate via speaking, try writing your ideas either in sentences or just using the key words. Generally speaking, most Japanese can read English better than they can listen to it, so it might be worthwhile to keep a small pad and pen in your pocket if you're worried about speaking.

Remember that humor is the most difficult concept to translate. A lot of humor depends on wordplay, and even advanced students of English have trouble comprehending puns and other similar jokes. Japanese people do enjoy laughing — in fact they seem to think a sense of humor is every foreigner's strong point — but the humor has to be kept simple, either through gestures, facial expressions, or sheer silliness.

COMMUNICATING IN JAPANESE

You may have just gotten off the airplane and, after being complimented on how well you could say "good afternoon" and "thank you" in Japanese, be lulled into a sense of how easy it is to learn the language.

Don't be.

Employees of the U.S. State Department who study Japanese require 1,410 hours of study to obtain what is labeled "limited working proficiency" — far, far more than those of other foreign languages such as Spanish or French. The main reason, of course, is the writing system; it takes many, many hours of study to be able to read a simple daily newspaper. As beautiful as *kanji* may appear to the eye — and they are beautiful — they also comprise one of the clumsiest writing systems in the world. But even the Chinese make do with only *kanji*. In Japan, however, there are *five* different writing systems in use: *kanji*, *hiragana*, *katakana*, Roman letters, and Arabic numerals — and these are all mixed together willy-nilly.

Then there is the initially confusing sentence structure (verbs go to the end of a sentence), the total lack of the future tense and plurals, and sentences which seem to have no subject whatsoever.

Intimidated? I'm not finished. Japanese also has varying degrees of politeness, without which the educated person is still just a rube. It's not just foreigners who have their work cut out for them; native Japanese spend many school years studying *kanji*, and even college graduates find they have to school themselves in the intricacies of politeness in order to perform in their new jobs.

That's the bad news. The good news is that Japanese, unlike Chinese, is not tonal and is relatively easy for newcomers to pronounce. More importantly, while reading and writing Japanese may be a Herculean feat, listening and speaking are not. With some serious effort, you can be reasonably conversant. Note the word *serious*; some books bill themselves as being able to teach Japanese to busy people — beware of such claims! If you've got time for self-study, you can find a listing of books I've found helpful over the years at the end of this book.

For sheer survival, you should master *katakana* and *hiragana* as quickly as you can. Virtually all words of foreign origin are written with *katakana*, so without knowing them you won't be able to find your favorite foods on a restaurant menu. *Kanji* can come later. At the very least you should learn how to write your own address correctly.

When speaking, remember to stretch your vowels where necessary and hit your double consonants. If you don't, you may find yourself easily misunderstood. One friend of mine told his colleagues about his trip to Beppu, only to find that they couldn't understand exactly where he'd been. In rising and falling intonations he mightily tried. "Beppu. Beppu? Beppu! BEPPU!" He believes they eventually got it.

For people who want to attend a language class, they can be found in practically every major city, and usually at reasonable rates. Check with your local community resources. Or you can find someone who will swap 30 minutes of English conversation for 30 minutes of Japanese conversation. However, these sometimes seem to degenerate into English-only lessons, apparently to the relief of both speakers.

The Japanese government sponsors an annual test to measure foreigners' understanding of Japanese. Known as the Japanese Language Proficiency Test (*Nihongo Nouryoku Shiken*), it is given on the first Sunday of December at a few sites in Japan, as well as at selected locations abroad. Applications are available from major bookstores in the late summer for a few hundred yen; the application itself requires a fee of about 5,000 yen. Note that Level 4 is the easiest level; it requires basic grammar and listening skills and requires the knowledge of about 100 *kanji*. The listening and grammar get progressively more difficult, and the *kanji* more numerous. Level 3 requires an understanding of about 300 *kanji*; Level 2, 1,000 kanji; and Level 1, all of the 1,945 *kanji* required of the typical Japanese high school graduate. The test consumes the better part of the day. For more information, check the following website: **www.aiej.or.jp/ examination/jlpt_e.html.**

It wouldn't be Japan if there weren't a multitude of tests to be taken. There is also the JETRO Business Japanese Proficiency Test, a one-level pass-fail exam to test a foreigner's ability to understand Japanese in business situations. More information can be found at **www.jetro.go.jp/it/e/bj/info/howto.html**. Finally, there is the *Kanken*, a *kanji* test originally intended for Japanese people but now becoming increasingly popular with non-Japanese as well. It is given three times annually. For more information, go to **www.kanken.or.jp**.

FORMS OF ADDRESS

In the Japanese language, surnames are followed by given names. However, most Japanese will reverse that order when writing their names in Roman letters. Thus, 田中二郎 (Tanaka Jirou) becomes "Jirou Tanaka" in communications with English speakers. There is no real reason why the Japanese should do that. The Chinese don't change their name order for anyone; 毛澤東 (Mao Zedong) in Chinese is still "Mao Zedong" in English. However, at present that's what most Japanese do.

Japanese people typically address each other by their surnames, especially while at work. This is true even among longtime friends. Do not think you are breaking the ice and creating a friendlier atmosphere by addressing people by their given names; all you're doing is embarrassing them in front of their colleagues. Take a cue from what the people around you appreciate and respect.

Also, when directly addressing someone, Japanese will usually add the honorific suffix *–san*. This can be used for either men or women; it is equivalent to the English Mr. or Ms. The title *–sama* is used in very polite situations and *–sensei* is the all-purpose honorific for an educated person, usually a teacher. In personal situations, you can use *–kun,* a personal term of endearment for boys, while *–chan* does the same thing for women. Do not use a title when talking about yourself. I wouldn't refer to myself as "Mr. Sean" in English; neither should I say I am "Sean-*san*".

Differentiations are also made between one's own lousy things and another's highly exalted things. When talking about my own wife I use the simple word *tsuma*, but when talking about someone else's wife I use the more respectful *okusan*. There is also the honorific prefix *–o*, which is used as a marker in front of words that describe the important things of daily life, such as tea (*o-cha*) and room (*o-heya*). Do not get carried away with this and start creating new compounds, however.

CONVERSING WITH THE JAPANESE

In most situations Japanese people are physically reserved; there is no hearty backslapping or wild gesticulation going on here. Moreover, Japanese typically talk to each other in what most non-Japanese would consider to be muted voices. Speaking at what you might think to be an acceptable volume would likely draw stares from other people around you, who might be as shocked by your loudness as much as the fact that you are speaking a foreign language. On a crowded train, you may discover that someone who is quite friendly to you at work may be reluctant to speak to you, merely so as not to draw attention to himself.

Japanese are also the world's leaders at artfully avoiding conversations. You may be surprised that that friendly co-worker in your office will try to slip past you in public without you noticing him. If you flag him down and try to speak to him, you may begin to notice a reluctance on his part to enthusiastically join you in conversation. Perhaps this is due to his embarrassment about his limited English ability, or perhaps because he is generally uneasy around foreigners, or perhaps because he really doesn't like you as much as you thought he did. Nevertheless, he will stay and talk with you, hoping that you will quickly understand his feeling and release him from any further social burden.

It is rare, though not impossible, to meet someone who approaches you and asks, "May I practice speaking English with you?" However, you may from time to time notice people who attempt to adroitly practice their listening skills by eavesdropping on your conversation with someone else. Remember that, in general, speaking is the worst communication skill for many Japanese; there are more people who can listen well than speak well. Use discretion and don't air your personal issues in front of everyone who rides the train!

INDIRECT COMMUNICATION

As most of you have probably heard, the Japanese are remarkably talented at talking all around a topic without ever actually zeroing in on it. One renowned linguist, whose lecture I suffered through, compared the Western speaking style as moving in a direct line from Point A to Point B, while the Japanese start at a point on the periphery and slowly wind inward in a series of ever-smaller concentric circles. As one might guess, this takes an awful lot of time to accomplish, with the accompanying increase in verbiage. More than once I have interrupted a lengthy conversation by saying, with just more than a bit of exasperation, "Look! Just say what it is you want to say!"

Why do the Japanese do this? Well, one reason is that it is absolutely, undoubtedly politer. The speaker can do the appropriate amount of verbal stroking of the listener, and he can gauge the effect of his words on the listener as he slowly glides toward the topic. The speaker and the listener in effect work together, neither insulting each other's intelligence nor leaving anything assumed.

Sometimes the cues can be easy to pick up. One Japanese woman I know asked a British friend of mine if he'd heard any news recently. No, he hadn't, and he was puzzled as to why that question had popped out of the blue. Suddenly it hit him, and he asked her, "Have *you* heard any news recently?" She was grateful that he had provided her the opportunity to speak, and proceeded to regale him with the latest gossip she'd heard.

There is another, warier reason for all of the indirectness: the less explicit information one says, the less one gives away. In situations where it is obvious that one person has all the power over another, conversations can be surprisingly blunt and direct. Most negotiations, however, are anything but obvious, and so talk can sometimes be merely a façade, a game in which each speaker is waiting for the other to make a mistake and give something of value away. This can be just as true in intra-company communication as in inter-company communication; Japanese office politics can be deadly, as different factions slowly assemble and try to find each other's weak points.

Politeness can go a long way, but nevertheless most Westerners will find communicating with Japanese people frustrating at one time or another. Do not, however, make the mistake of believing that other Japanese don't get frustrated communicating with each other, either. My wife once answered a phone call at her office, and was informed that Mr. A and Mr. B would be attending the upcoming meeting. She passed the message along to her supervisor.

"Did he say if Mr. C and Mr. D were going to the meeting?" asked her supervisor.

"No, he just said Mr. A and Mr. B were going," answered my wife.

"But he didn't say anything about Mr. C and Mr. D?"

"No, he didn't."

After a moment, my wife's supervisor started wondering aloud: "I wonder why they didn't say anything about Mr. C and Mr. D."

Another person might have been privately stewing at that point: *What is it you're trying to say—do you want me to call them back and find out or what?* Of course my wife could never even begin to say such a thing to her boss. But you should certainly keep in mind that there are many Japanese too who get impatient with all of the conversational proprieties that are required in Japanese society. The flip side to all of this is that, because many Japanese believe English-speaking societies to be more direct than their own, they will sometimes speak English with an almost embarrassing frankness.

You should also be careful of what you say—hints are often enough. One student of mine invited my father and me to her house for lunch. We talked for a while and then, just before setting lunch on the table, she asked him what food he liked. He casually replied that he loved fried shrimp. Now, I knew she had made a large lunch, but fried shrimp was not one of the things on the menu. Yet in the few minutes that my father was in the washroom, *boom*—shrimp came out of the freezer and were quickly fried. My father thought it all a nice coincidence.

JAPANESE ENGLISH

Despite the problems that many Japanese have with English, there are oodles and scads of shop signs, menus, T-shirts, pamphlets, and what all written in English. Some of these are professionally checked, but a good many aren't. My favorite misspelling is a common one: a beauty salon is often referred to as a "hair saloon". It makes me imagine a wrangler removing his 10-gallon hat, only to reveal a perfect 10-gallon coiffure. "Looking *good*, cowboy!"

While amusing, try to keep it in perspective. At least most people are trying to communicate in English, even if you sometimes can't figure out the reason why they're bothering. But trying they are, so just appreciate the effort.

NONVERBAL COMMUNICATION

Even though the Japanese are a physically reserved people, they do communicate via gestures, albeit more subtly.

For example, if a man wants to demonstrate that he is thinking, he will cross his arms and tuck his chin into his chest. If he wants to gesture to himself, he will point, not to his chest, but to his nose. If he wants to signal to you to come closer to him, he will gesture with the palm of his hand down, not up—do not be mistaken in thinking it means "go away"! And if he wants to slip past you in a cramped place, he will karate-chop the air—apparently the effort involved in saying "excuse me" would be too much.

If a shop is closed, or if something cannot be done, a person will gesture with his forearms crossed in an "X". The same "x" done with the index finger of both hands is used to ask for the bill at a restaurant. A gesture of "no" can be done by waving one hand in front of the face, fingers pointing up, as if trying to fan a bad smell away. Money can be indicated by making the Western sign for "OK", but with the palm of the hand facing upward. Counting with one's fingers can be done with one hand: The numbers one to five are counted by bending the fingers of one hand inward, while six to 10 are figured by then extending those same fingers outward. And the ubiquitous peace sign shows up in *every* photograph.

A closed fist with only the pinky extended means "girlfriend", while one thumb up sometimes means "boyfriend." A closed fist over the nose, with rolled index finger and thumb inward, means "stuck-up". And the pulling down of the skin under one eye, with tongue extended, is a childish gesture that might roughly be translated as "Bleah!"

To show polite attention to what you are saying, people will never put food or drink into their mouths while you are talking to them. If someone is lifting a cup to his mouth, be polite and wait for him to finish sipping before resuming speaking, because otherwise he'll start to put the cup down and never finish his drink.

My particular favorite, however, is the expression of "what you ask is absolutely impossible, but I can't directly admit as much." It's the sound of air inhaled through the mouth, a sucking of the teeth — the more incredible your request, the more oxygen will be drained from the room.

–Chapter Twelve–

CULTURE AND TRADITIONS

"Nothing is more hallowing than the union of kindred spirits in art."

–Okakura Kakuzo, *The Book of Tea*

RELIGION

The native religion of Japan is Shintou. Shintou is an indigenous folk religion that finds spirits abounding in nature. There is no formal creed, or indeed much of any philosophy behind it. It basically allows followers a way of currying favor with various gods so as to receive good luck. Even today, many older Japanese will, when walking past a shrine, turn and bow to the spirits within.

Mahayana Buddhism arrived in Japan in the sixth century. Over the centuries it grew in prestige and divided into sects. Today the most well-known forms of Japanese Buddhism are Souka Gakkai, the quasi-political religious group that has significant political clout, and Zen Buddhism.

Shintou and Buddhism have a long and intertwined history in

Japan, and it is only in the past hundred years or so that they have been separated. Even today things can be confusing, as the design of Shintou shrines and Buddhist temples can look very much alike. The key tip: If there's a *torii* (a large, two-legged arch) standing at the entrance of the grounds, it's a Shintou shrine; if not, it's a Buddhist temple.

A visit to a shrine first involves the visitor washing his hands and mouth at a pool in front of the shrine. Then he will make an offering of money, ring the gong, bow twice, clap twice, and bow twice more.

To an outsider's eyes, there are a few differences about religion as it is practiced in Japan. The most obvious is that in Japan it is perfectly permissible—indeed, almost expected—that people can be both a Buddhist and Shintoist at the same time. Many Japanese, for example, will get married in a Shintou ceremony, but will have Buddhist rites at their funerals.

Too many Buddhist and Shintou priests get their jobs simply because they are following in the father's footsteps. One American I know, a practitioner of Zen, was invited into a Buddhist priest's house. The priest was impressed by the American's diligence and wanted to talk with him further. He offered the American a cigarette and a glass of whiskey, and when he politely declined the priest smoked and drank by himself. As they talked, the American's eyes wandered, noticing the large collection of adult videos on the bookshelf and the expensive car outside—and it was all nothing the priest was ashamed of whatsoever.

In fact, many Japanese seem to avoid people who appear overtly religious. Occasionally you will meet a proselytizer of some religion on the street, but in general people seem to think that that kind of behavior is reserved for cult members. People have strong memories of the cult that killed and injured so many people on the Tokyo subways with toxic sarin gas in 1995, and find anyone who is not moderate in his religion a little unsettling.

Performing dispassionate, ritualistic acts is fine, I suppose, but many Japanese cannot begin to fathom those who take strong moral stands. So much of Japanese society is geared for enjoying oneself in this world that there seems to be no appetite left for considering intangible issues. As one Japanese told me when I expressed an appreciation in the aesthetics of Zen, "I can't do it. It's just too hard." This attitude may go a long way in explaining why non-Japanese friends of mine who were so interested in Buddhism wound up criticizing Japan as a religiously dead society.

THE SEASONS

Japan has four seasons. Now this is not unusual. What *is* unusual, though, is how many people believe that Japan is very unique in having four distinct seasons. Some Japanese even find it hard to believe that other countries could be equally blessed. I knew one British woman who tried to gently point out that the English also experienced four seasons. "No, you don't," retorted her Japanese colleague.

Nevertheless, as befitting a society in which farmers have a political impact all out of proportion to their numbers, the changing of the seasons does hold particular meaning for all Japanese. The problem is that two of the four seasons can be quite brutal. Winters, heavily influenced by Siberian cold fronts to the north, can leave you feeling that you're never warm enough, even in your own apartment. Meanwhile, summers would be all right if you could spend all your days in shorts and T-shirts, but if you have to wear a tie or a dress, they can be disgustingly, drippingly hot and humid. Yet I have found that a jacket or a cardigan sweater is still essential for many people in summertime. Why? Well, look around you the next time you sit down in a restaurant. It's apparent that public air conditioners have only two settings in Japan: "Off" and "Maximum Polar Blast."

Accordingly, one of the most common conversation openers in Japan is "It's cold, isn't it?" (*"Samui desu ne."*) or "It's hot, isn't it?" (*"Atsui desu ne."*) You can indicate your agreement by saying *"So desu ne.*" Freethinker that I am, though, I often playfully try to point out that it's not really cold or hot, but rather merely cool or warm—just wait till the extreme weather kicks in! I do this partly because it seems that Japanese are never comfortable. Anything less than 21 degrees Celsius and they are cold; anything above 22 degrees Celsius and they are hot. For a country that has such wide seasonal variation, it does seem a shame that most people don't enjoy 95 percent of the weather available.

Spring and summer are very lovely, though, and the country is bewitchingly beautiful at this time. Spring, of course, is of primary importance as that is when the cherry trees blossom white and pink for an all-too-brief moment. That is followed by flowers of every sort which are planted in regular rows with loving care. I have seen beautiful spreads of flowers adjacent to busy highways where they would draw at most a cursory look; a flash of riotous color and then they would be gone. Yet culturally plants are important. People who have trouble naming four-legged animals and could not tell you the difference between an alligator and a crocodile will still be able to identify all different sorts of flowers and trees.

For my money, though, the best season is fall: golden days touched by a legacy of summer sunshine, but leavened with a bitingly cool breeze that has just appeared from around the corner. The changing of the leaves is as important here as it is in many other countries, and in Japan there's one short and nifty word to sum this up: *kouyou*. Fall sports many days without rain, just pure, clear blue skies.

JAPANESE CULTURE A TO Z

Bonsai

Bonsai is the technique of reducing a plant (usually but not always a pine tree) to its miniaturized essence. It is very remarkable and I marvel each time I see it, but every time someone gives me a *bonsai* for my own I haven't the heart to keep it whacked to size.

191

Calligraphy

Known as *shodou*, calligraphy is one of Japan's most important arts. The quality of one's handwriting has long been esteemed, and the brush strokes of famous people are highly valued. The study of calligraphy has an added bonus for Westerners, since it also helps in learning the *kanji* themselves.

Castles

Japan, of course, has many castles that stand as testimony to its warrior past. Most of them are reconstructed out of the finest ferro-concrete; a few, such as Himeji Castle in Hyogo prefecture, remain remarkable treasures. Any of them make for pleasurable exploring.

WHITE CASTLE. *Although mostly reconstructed, castles make fun visiting.*

BEST OF BOTH WORLDS. *At a typical graduation ceremony, parents, teachers, and graduates may dress up in fancy tuxedoes and dresses or in kimono.*

Clothing

Sadly, modern Japan has given up on traditional clothes in favor of Western styles, or of even attempting to work elements of established Japanese design into contemporary clothes.

The *kimono* is the most well-known garment of Japan. It can be made of silk or wool (for winter wear) or cotton (for summer). The *kimono* for men are black; those for women are printed in a variety of colors. *Kimono* are bound around the waist by a sash known as an *obi*. *Kimono* can be ordered new from a store for something less than the cost of your college education, or you can check out used kimono shops (such as are found in Kyoto) for some spectacular deals.

Other traditional clothes include *hakama*, a long skirt worn over a *kimono*; *yukata*, a simple cotton robe worn in summer and at resorts; and *happi*, a short cloak mostly worn by store employees during a sale.

Flower Arranging

Known as *ikebana*, flower arranging is beautiful when done correctly. It is also an art that many companies will, in the unthinking sexist manner that they have, assume that every young office lady knows.

Fortune Telling

All in all, the Japanese are a very superstitious people. Palm readers, known as *tesou-uranai*, are but one manifestation of this trait. Palm readers and tarot card readers come out at night, when they set up small tables near major stations and tell people, mostly women, their fortunes.

Games

The classic Japanese game of *go*, also known as *igo*, is easy to learn but impossibly difficult to master. Currently the world's best computers can beat the world's best chess players, but there is no computer yet that can top the best human being at *go*.

Shougi is the chess of Japan. It is also fun to play but may take a little bit longer to learn, since the pieces can only be identified by their complicated *kanji*.

Gardens

Whether large or small, a Japanese garden (*teien*) is laid out to provide the maximum viewing enjoyment possible. Some may be crowded but many others will be serenely peaceful, particularly on weekdays. Go and take your time.

Martial Arts

Martial arts, of course, are one of any Westerner's first impressions of the cultures of the Far East, and Japan is where many of them started. The subject is much larger than can be adequately treated in this book; however, a few points are in order.

There are two sorts of martial arts in Japan today: those that end in *-jitsu*, and those that end in *-dou*. The *-jitsu* ending implies a sport whose main point is combat; the ending *-dou*, meanwhile, refers to a sport that is teaching a certain "way" of being. The difference in nomenclature came about because the Occupation authorities frowned upon anything that seemed too martial, and in order to survive many schools changed their names and usually (though not always) changed their teachings. Thus, *jujitsu*, a favorite of hyperactive U.S. President Teddy Roosevelt, now exists alongside the newer *judou*. *Jujitsu* is a martial art in which the practitioners learn to grapple with and throw their opponents; *judou* is simply the competitive form of those same techniques.

The same applies to *kenjitsu*, which is traditional Japanese swordsmanship; more common today is *kendou*, which is the Japanese equivalent of fencing, albeit in this case with a bamboo stick called a *shinai*. Another related martial art is *iaidou*, which like *kenjitsu* uses traditional Japanese swords called *katana*. *Iaidou*, though it does have the *-dou* ending, seems to have skated right under the Occupation authorities' noses and preserved its integrity while only changing its name. The only main difference between *kenjitsu* and *iaidou* is that *kenjitsu* practices techniques with swords that are already drawn, while *iaidou* also teaches how to correctly draw and resheathe one's sword as well.

Other Japanese martial arts include *kyuudou* (Japanese archery); *shourinji kempo* (essentially the Japanese version of kung fu); and *aikido*, which is less about combat and more about defensive moves to protect oneself from an attacker. Finally, the most famous of all Japanese martial arts is probably *karate*, which really isn't Japanese at all but Okinawan. *Karate* teaches how to strike and punch; the art was considered so lethal that for many years the Japanese government authorities forbade *karate* entirely. Only by secretly practicing in the temples of Okinawa could the teachers of *karate* hand down lessons to the next generation.

Paper

Paper is more than paper here—it's yet another subtly refined art. (Which might explain why so many are reluctant to clear piles of it off their desks.) It is called *washi* and can be found at better stationery shops.

Pottery and Lacquerware

Pottery (*setomono*) is one of the outstanding examples of Japanese craftsmanship. It can range from the simple *wabisabi* styles of old Kyoto to the finest porcelain of Arita, near Nagasaki. You can get the best prices on pottery at dealer outlets.

With its hues of red and black, lacquerware (*shikki*) is one of the top arts of Japan. It is the art of colorfully protecting carved wood. You can find examples of this throughout Japan, but the lacquerware of Kanazawa is especially notable.

Theater

Kabuki is song and dance, drama and comedy. It can be initially daunting, particularly in its use of *onnagata* (men performing female roles). But with just a little knowledge of the play you can have a good time. Thankfully, many companies will provide an English synopsis of the performance, which may put you one up on your Japanese friends as they are expected to have no difficulties comprehending 17th-century Japanese.

Nou is Japanese theater that predates *kabuki*. It is relatively harder to find a performance of *nou*, as *nou* is far more static than the fun-loving *kabuki*. It may also be a bit much to sit through an entire performance, as it may last several hours and your attention span may begin wandering after a while. Still, it's worth checking out at least once.

Bunraku is Japan's puppet theater. It is preserved at the National Bunraku Theater in Osaka. You may also be able to catch a performance in Tokyo or at the theater's annual road show.

Takarazuka is Japan's all-female theater. It is very popular with young and middle-aged women.

Sumo

Japan's classic wrestling is more than a sport; it is also tinged with the religious symbolism of Shintou. It takes place at a tournament called a *basho* which is held over a period of 15 days, beginning and ending on Sunday. There are six tournaments a year (January, May, and September in Tokyo; March in Osaka; July in Nagoya; and November

WANT SUMOU? *Sumou wrestlers prepare for an exhibition match held in a small community.*

in Fukuoka) plus you can catch practice matches in Tokyo or an exhibition somewhere else in the country. The rules are quite simple, really; two wrestlers grapple with each other until one is either ejected from the ring or touches the ground with any part of his body other than his feet. Once you get over the sight of two nearly naked, overweight men strutting around, it can be a lot of fun. A lot of foreigners find themselves taking to *sumou* rather quickly.

There is some concern recently that *sumou* may be waning in popularity. The retirements of top-ranked stars such as U.S.-born Akebono and Konishiki (who topped out at 275 kg) and the Japanese brother duo of Takanohana and Wakanohana have left a void for many fans. It is now rare to see a tournament sold out for its entire duration. There has been a growing increase in wrestlers from Mongolia, but they haven't stirred the same passions as the Japan–U.S. showdowns of a decade ago. Ominously, young boys are becoming less interested in going through the necessary training to become a wrestler. A major makeover in the sport seems likely one day.

Tea Ceremony

Tea ceremony (*sadou*) is perhaps the highest of Japan's traditional arts. Moreover, it incorporates elements from other Japanese arts, such as flower arranging and calligraphy, so that a lesson in tea ceremony covers a broad cultural spectrum.

A complete demonstration in tea ceremony can take up to six hours, but that is a rare event that will occur not even once a year. Should you be fortuitous enough to participate in such a ceremony, you will be treated to such rituals as the contemplation of a garden, a brief meditation before a special object (e.g., a scroll of stylized calligraphy), an examination of the utensils used during the ceremony itself, and an extensive meal. Of course, there is also tea!

While green tea is common in daily life in Japan, the tea used in tea ceremony will be a thicker variety known as *matcha*. Actually,

TEA TIME. Traditionally attired, a young woman prepares green tea for a sadou *ceremony.*

there are also different kinds of *matcha*. When I attended a tea ceremony, I was warned to expect the thick variety. "No worries," I said. "I've had it before."

Unfortunately, what I thought was the thick *matcha* turned out to be the thin variety. When the thick variety was finally introduced, I could not believe its color and consistency. It looked exactly like green ketchup. But I remembered 1-2-3, so I drank a first sip, a second sip—and then gagged on the third. I wonder if I could politely decline next time by saying, "Honestly, it's not my cup of tea."

The one drawback of tea ceremony for Westerners, however, is that it requires you to kneel on the straw mat floor of the tea ceremony room (the position is called *seiza*). Some schools are very strict about this and require you to kneel for the entire time; others take a more relaxed approach and let the men sit cross-legged and the women with their legs to the side. However, for even the more relaxed schools, you should make an effort to assume the kneeling position for the presentation of the tea itself, as well as the elements associated with the tea that are presented—even the tea menu! Once they are passed to the next person, you can resume a more comfortable position.

Tea ceremony today is largely the province of women, who have comparatively more free time to pursue club activities than do men. However, originally tea ceremony was the domain of men, particularly the samurai who devised the intricate rituals associated with it.

LEARNING JAPANESE ARTS

It is very possible to learn Japanese arts by studying with a teacher or by participating in a club. There are countless organizations which are very happy to teach foreigners; just ask around.

If you are inclined to participate in a club that practices a Japanese art, be aware that most clubs expect something more than a casual commitment. The foreigner who participates only once a month in a club that meets weekly is neither completely respected nor fully considered a member of the group. Like most groups in Japan, respect is partially derived from constantly participating in all of the group's activities. You should ask yourself whether you can make such a commitment, or something approximating it.

If you're interested in a club, but feel daunted by the demands that it might make on your time, you could start by telling the club that you'd like to join for a period of time—say six or three months—to get a feel for the club's routine. During that time you should be able to fairly assess whether you like what you are learning and whether you like your fellow classmates.

Chapter Thirteen

RECREATION

"If someone asked me what a human being ought to devote the maximum of his time to, I would answer, 'training.' Train more than you sleep."

–Oyama Masutatsu, judo master

The question persists: How can so many recreational diversions continue to exist in a country where people are rumored to do nothing except work all the time? Somebody has obviously missed something!

One thing to keep in mind: When tackling recreational activities, the Japanese apply the same intensity that they do to their jobs. I've seen couples who would spend weekends every month in the park, getting ready for an annual festival—by practicing the three-legged race. And I've seen hikers head out on a day hike that wouldn't tax a tenderfoot, but they were nevertheless outfitted with walking sticks, backpacks, water bottles, and lederhosen. Really. And a green felt cap with a feather stuck in it. *Really!*

So remember that, if you plan to do something with your Japanese friends, your clothing and your attitude should demonstrate your seriousness about your hobby. And, if you play a sport, remember that there's very little of this "we're just here to have a good time" nonsense—most everyone plays hard to win.

BEACHES AND WATER ACTIVITIES

Going to the beach in Japan is invariably a disappointment. The beaches may not have the wonderfully silky sand found in Southeast Asia, but they would be perfectly acceptable—were it not for the garbage. Whether washed up on shore or left behind by thoughtless visitors, trash accumulates on many of Japan's beaches. Yet what is truly amazing, even scary, is how a young family can sit themselves down on the sand, right amongst the plastic bags and discarded beer cans and other, more disgusting items—and pretend that it is a pleasurable experience.

You should also be aware that, just because you see people cavorting in the surf, it does not mean that the water would pass safety standards in your home country. There's a fine beach right in the heart of the city near where I live, but I know very few foreigners who think the water is safe for swimming. Farther away from the city, the sea looks much more pleasant and would make for enjoyable swimming, were it not for the aforementioned garbage that litters the walk to the water.

Should you have the opportunity to escape to one of Japan's islands, you will undoubtedly find beaches much more to your liking. Some trash will likely be visible even here, but overall the experience is far more pleasing. Some may have cabins to rent or other facilities for group activities.

Oddly, many Japanese would never dream of swimming in the sea outside of the "swimming season", which lasts roughly from the time school lets out (21 July) to the end of *o-bon* (15 August), when the jellyfish are usually expected to make their appearance. If you go swimming on a hot day outside of that season, you may have much of the beach to yourself.

Surfing is popular among younger Japanese. Many locations offer reasonable surfing conditions, although the best surfing is reputed to be found off the coast of Miyazaki prefecture. Scuba diving is also popular; there are many diving shops where you can rent quality equipment, albeit not cheaply. Scuba diving courses and licenses can be expensive—if you don't already have a license, you might want to take care of that before you arrive. Alternatively, you can take a holiday in another country such as Thailand and get your license there. Jet skis can be rented at many popular waterfront locations. Some places even have paragliding.

Fishing

For the man who just wants to chuck it all and get out of the office, fishing is the dream escape. Some men head out virtually every weekend, either to the sea on small boats or to mountain rivers. Although almost certainly not as popular as pachinko, fishing provides salaried workers with a touchstone to Japan's traditional past. This nostalgia is further nurtured in a comic film series, *Tsuri Baka Nisshi*, which tells about a man so in love with fishing that everything else in his life suffers.

GATEBALL

Gateball is a variation of croquet played on a dirt field. It is popular with older people. Take it from me, the old ladies are competitive!

GOLF

As you might have guessed, golf in a country the size of Japan is an extremely expensive activity—perhaps not as expensive as it was during the bubble economy, but still not cheap. Though many golf clubs nationwide are ailing, it is still entirely possible that you could buy a round-trip ticket from Tokyo to Honolulu and spend the weekend golfing there, and still come out ahead over what you might pay at the priciest courses in Japan.

Golf is the favored sport of businessmen who would like to spend time together and strengthen personal relationships. Recently, an increasing number of women can also be seen on the courses, as they tend to have more free time than their workaholic husbands.

Most businessmen who itch to practice their golf swing do so either at driving ranges in the city (identifiable by their fortresses of wire mesh), or on train platforms. I've seen many guys who were waiting for the next local train execute a spectacular drive. Without clubs, of course.

HIKING AND CAMPING

The mountains and countryside of Japan can be stupendously gorgeous, and trails exist for both the experienced mountaineer and the novice hiker. Put on a good pair of shoes, grab your daypack, and go.

HOT SPRINGS

If the text in guidebooks could be highlighted with neon signs, I would do so for hot springs. Japan's hot springs (*onsen*) are one of the most outstanding features of the country. No matter whether you stay 10 days or 10 years, you should definitely make a visit to a hot spring part of your stay in Japan.

Hot springs come in all different shapes and sizes. There are still a few of the old-fashioned public baths (*sentou*), which date from a time when individuals did not have private bathing facilities. There are the modern hotels with whole floors dedicated to various kinds of baths: hot baths, warm baths, cold baths, Jacuzzi baths, baths laden with mineral salts, and so on. Finally, there are the traditional baths with matching accommodation, usually a *ryokan*. These last can almost always be visited without making a reservation for the night (which can be very expensive, but worth it if you can afford it at least once!)

Traditional baths are usually found in the countryside and in the mountains, although a few entrepreneurs have done a remarkable job of recreating rural ambience at locations in the hearts of the cities. Like many things in Japan, there is a certain etiquette necessary. As with all bathing in Japan, wash and rinse your body completely before stepping into the bath; the bath is merely meant for relaxing in. And no, people don't wear swimsuits but merely take a small white towel with them to cover their privates while walking naked. When sitting in the bath, many people will fold the towel and place it atop their heads. And remember that this is supposed to be relaxing—don't try to rush through the whole experience! Take your time washing, soaking, and thinking.

One last point, which is probably obvious: Some hotels offer radon baths which, as the name implies, is an enclosed room where one can take a bath in radon-laced water. Radon is alleged to have medicinal properties, but as one doctor confided to me, so many people in Japan are worried about nuclear proliferation and the dangers of atomic energy, yet they'll unquestioningly jump into a bath where the radioactivity is out of control. My advice: Stay away.

KARAOKE

I'm sure most people know what this is, even if the original Japanese pronunciation is completely at odds with the English one. In the past decade *karaoke* seems to have slipped in popularity, which makes a perfect answer for your friends who think nothing ever gets better in this world. There are few "social" activities more constricting than going to a semi-darkened room and listening to one person sing loudly (and badly) while everyone else ignores him and shuffles through a book to look up the song they'll sing next. Once a year is enough for me.

In yet another sign of the social apocalypse awaiting Japan, *karaoke* parlors are reporting an increase in people who check in for a few hours to sing by themselves.

MAH-JONGG

This table game brought over from China is the other most popular form of gambling. In a way it's not unlike poker, although it's played with tiles instead of cards. And like poker it can be played strictly for fun or very small stakes. Naturally, it is mostly played all night by men interested in serious gambling.

MUSEUMS

Museums housing Japanese treasures are generally rewarding as they should be. Museums housing works by non-Japanese artists are usually less so; someone may have purchased a pencil sketch that Picasso did on the back of an envelope, and then built a two-story concrete block to house this "treasure". However, because of its relative wealth vis-à-vis the rest of the world, many wonderful art shows do pass through the country. Traveling exhibitions from Egypt, from Tibet, and from the British Museum, just to name a few, will enable you to see some of the most sumptuous works of art created by man.

Department stores and shopping malls will also have art exhibits, many of which focus on popular animated characters. Since these shows will "coincidentally" have a gift shop at the end selling mouse ears, enjoy at your own risk!

One thing I feel compelled to add is that there a lot of oddball museums in the hinterlands of Japan. I was driving around the mountains of Kumamoto when I stumbled across a museum dedicated to—I kid you not—Thomas Edison. Yes, the same Edison who was responsible for perfecting the light bulb and inventing the phonograph. It seems that one of the many minor religious cults in Japan has an almost superstitious regard for the power of electricity, and since Edison created so many wonderful devices powered by electricity, he is seen almost as a high priest of sacred knowledge. Weird.

PACHINKO AND SLOT MACHINES

Give a Japanese man some time off and there's probably one thing he wants to do more than any other: pachinko.

This vertical pinball game, not terribly exciting, is found in garishly lit parlors in big cities and tiny towns everywhere. Together with slot machines, they are Japan's main form of gambling, although of course people will be quick to point that gambling is illegal in Japan. What happens in pachinko is this: You buy a basket of small steel balls and sit down in front of the machine of your choice. Then, after feeding the balls into the machine, you use the game's knob to shoot the balls into certain holes in the machine. If you find the lucky holes, or if you can trigger the Vegas-style one-armed bandit videos in the newer machines, you will be rewarded with more steel balls than when you started playing. Fail to do these things, and you will see your collection of steel balls dwindle to nothing.

When you're finished—and be aware that many Japanese can spend endless hours at this game—you can exchange your balls at the counter for a small prize, say, a teddy bear. Then, after you leave the pachinko parlor, you go around the corner to a small window that just "happens" to exchange cash for teddy bears.

There is a wide array of Japanese cultural pursuits, whether in the traditional or the contemporary arts, and over the years I guess I have met at least one foreigner who has dug every one of them. But I'll be damned if I've ever met one Westerner who enjoyed pachinko, and I don't think I'm going to anytime soon, either. It's not just that the game is boring; it's also the fairly obvious indication that many pachinko parlors have criminal connections, and even more the distaste at the pachinko player's demeanor. Glassy-eyed and slack-jawed, unable to take his gaze away from the game, the winning player finds the correct way to turn that knob—and then holds it in place for as long as he can physically manage it. The pose of the typical pachinko player suggests nothing so much as a meditating Zen student who has emptied his mind of everything.

One further note: f you're driving around the countryside and just can't find a public toilet, stop and use the one at the easily spotted pachinko parlor. They have by far the cleanest, nicest toilets you'll find on your trip.

SKIING AND SNOWBOARDING

Skiing and snowboarding are very popular winter pastimes. Many Japanese first learned to ski while on a high school trip to a ski resort, and the country is blessed with many mountains on which they can continue to hone their skills.

ZOOS AND BOTANICAL GARDENS

Zoos are generally disappointing and saddening in Japan. Animals are kept in enclosures far too small, and their living conditions can appear shoddy indeed. And no, I don't think it is sufficient justification to say that Japanese people also have to live in cramped housing as well. By contrast, botanical gardens are well maintained and a real pleasure to see.

KYOTO AND NARA

If you're disappointed that you haven't found the Japan of your dreams in Tokyo, then by all means head over to Kyoto—you'll probably find it here.

Kyoto was Japan's capital a long time ago, and over the centuries it accumulated so many architectural treasures that today a tourist fairly trips over the numerous temples, shrines, and museums that stretch across the city. The city was spared any bombing during World War II, so most attractions are originals, not reconstructions as is so common elsewhere in Japan. It's the one place you shouldn't miss.

Although one should not choose it over its more famous cousin, Nara to me is a much more pleasant place to visit. It is smaller and quieter. Just be sure to be careful of the deer; they're cute, but they also are surprisingly aggressive if they think you've got snacks for them.

HIROSHIMA AND NAGASAKI

These two cities, to date, are the only ones in the world to have experienced the horrors of atomic weapons. Today, of course, there is no visible damage apart from a few symbolic structures left standing. That, and the wounds of the sufferers who survived—and the scars in their families' hearts. No matter one's feelings about the bombs, one cannot but feel empathy with the ordinary people who lived or died on 6 and 9 August 1945. Both cities have museums documenting those horrific events, and though some displays have a

REMEMBER. *"Rest in peace, for we will not repeat the mistake," reads the silent monument to the dead at Hiroshima.*

tinge of anti-Americanism, there is also implicit regret that the country's wartime leaders led the country down that fiery path. Either city makes a compelling and sobering visit.

MOUNT FUJI

Like the Eiffel Tower for France and the Great Wall for China, Mount Fuji stands as *the* symbol for Japan. And climbing Mount Fuji (*Fuji-san* in Japanese, <u>not</u> Fujiyama) is something that so many people, both Japanese and foreign, just feel they have to do. Being easily accessible from Tokyo, a lot of people take up the challenge.

Technically, you can climb Mount Fuji any time of the year,

although to do so in the winter would require the skills of Sir Edmund Hillary. Realistically, the climbing season for most people is restricted to July and August, when the snows have melted and the summit temperatures are merely chilly, not numbing. Mount Fuji stands 3,776 meters (12,388 feet) high, and what may start out as a balmy summer day at the base can quickly turn into a beautiful January day at the top. Be prepared; stick a sweatshirt or windbreaker into your daypack.

Good shoes are also recommended, as well as a flashlight. Traditionally, most people start their climb after nightfall in order to see the sunrise from the top of the mountain. At night, the parade of hikers carrying their torches forms an elegant snake of light as far as one can see. And though the path upward is anything but treacherous, it is a mountain nevertheless and deserves to be treated with respect. A friend of a friend died on Mount Fuji, merely because of his own cocky carelessness. Caution is certainly merited.

Not wanting to do things like everyone else, I started my climb from the famous fifth way-station at 12:30 p.m., wanting to see sunset from the top. Or, to put it another way, I had no desire to climb a mountain in the dark. I was reasonably fit at the time, although admittedly the only hiking training I had done beforehand was stepping over sararimen passed out on train platforms. Regardless, I found the trek to be hard but not overly demanding, and with short breaks I reached the top in 5 1/2 hours.

Drinks and food were available along the way, and they appeared to be absurdly overpriced, until I stopped and considered the effort it took to drag the stuff up there in the first place. Additionally, I passed many hikers who paid good money for snorts from oxygen tanks. Some people do complain of altitude sickness, but I personally didn't experience any problems, and I came away feeling it was yet another overrated danger in Japan.

My real concern, however, lay in going *down* the mountain in the dark, and I was extremely thankful that I'd brought my flashlight. It

DUSTY SLOG. *Climbing Mount Fuji isn't easy, but much of the path is wide and level.*

took 3 ¹/₂ hours to get down the mountain, and in truth it was much, much harder. For two days the tendons in my knees and ankles screamed with every step thereafter. Furthermore, I discovered upon reaching the fifth way-station that there is no public transport at that hour down the mountain. Sweaty and in agony, I found myself forlornly hitchhiking for any ride whatsoever, until one taxi driver took pity on me and cut me a really good deal to get to the nearest youth hostel.

The verdict? Seen from far away, Mount Fuji is a picturesque mountain. Up close, it is a dismal pile of gray ash and uninteresting rocks. There's nothing really to see—there are no trees whatsoever, and while the view is fine it is unremarkable. It has none of the poetic charm that clings to Chinese mountains such as Huangshan. It was fun once, but it would take a lot to get me up there once again. A Japanese proverb says that you're wise to climb Fuji once and foolish to do it twice; it is spot on as far as I'm concerned.

I have read many books about Japan, and I have found that there are people who try to read deep meanings into Japanese society, merely based upon their experiences while climbing Fuji. I don't know if I could make such a judgment; after all, it's only a mountain. I would simply say that, with the benefit of hindsight, I would have been better off climbing in the dark.

HOKKAIDO

Hokkaido is Japan's last frontier. Sparsely populated and wildly beautiful, it is blanketed with snow in the winter and plump with wild greenery in the summer. It's the place where families in minivans head for summer vacation. Bookings can be hard to get in peak season, so be sure to make reservations for lodging or campsites.

OKINAWA

There is no more relaxed place in Japan than Okinawa, and no people mellower than the Okinawans. This is despite the fact that, like Tibet, they have seen their culture trampled upon by outsiders. Historically, Okinawa was an independent entity known as the Ryukyu Kingdom, and it maintained as much contact with China as it did with Japan. First conquered by Japanese from the island of Kyushu, it has been absorbed into Japan, and young Okinawans today see themselves as Japanese as anyone from the four main islands. Nevertheless, they seem livelier and friendlier than other Japanese, and if there is an element of anger over their land being used for U.S. military bases, it is as much directed at the Japanese government for letting it happen as it is at the Americans themselves.

The swimming and diving on the main island are fine but nothing special; better venues for both can be found among the many islands that make up the Ryukyu chain from Okinawa down to nearly Taiwan.

Chapter Fourteen

EDUCATION

"While young, the tree can be easily bent."
–Japanese proverb

In Japan, there are both public and private schools. All public schools, and most private schools, are licensed as educational facilities by the Ministry of Education, Culture, Sports, Science and Technology. The ministry outlines basic goals and curriculum, and approves textbooks for school use. Over the years it has also exerted stronger control of schools. However, local boards of education and PTAs have some influence regarding curriculum, at least until the high school level.

Education is divided into six years of elementary schooling (*shougakkou*), three years of junior high school (*chuugakkou*), and three years of high school (*koutougakkou*). Elementary school is preceded by kindergarten, and high school is followed by a variety of two-year colleges and technical schools, four-year universities, six-year medical schools, and numerous post-graduate programs leading to doctoral degrees. Only elementary school and junior high school are compulsory, though nearly everyone attends high school as well.

The school calendar follows the same April-March calendar as businesses do. A child who will be seven years old between 1 April of one year and 31 March of the next is expected to enroll in first grade of elementary school. Skipping grades is unheard of; what matters is not a child's ability but his age.

Because of tough gun laws, parents do not have to fear that their children might not come home because they've been machine-gunned by their classmates. However, bullying is a severe problem. Called *ijime*, it usually occurs when a group of students decide to go after one particular student who is perceived to be different. Taunting, ostracism, and physical abuse are the most common forms of bullying. In the most tragic cases, bullying can lead to death, usually by the

NAZIS THEY'RE NOT. *Junior high school students salute their principal as they march prior to the school's sports festival.*

victim's own suicide. It is only then that principals and teachers realize how well they avoided the problem that was right in front of them all along. The demonstrations of remorse and contrition are impressive; it would be more impressive, however, if they had demonstrated some foresight in the first place.

To an absurd degree, Japanese society depends upon teachers training children correctly. If a student is in trouble with the law, the police will call the teacher before calling the parents. It seems that parents are meant to be cut out of the equation. A teacher I know had a conference with one mother at the family's house. While the child was in the next room watching TV, the mother told the teacher, "Please tell my child each day to do his homework as soon as he gets home from school." What the teacher REALLY wanted to say was, "Why don't you do it yourself!" But he couldn't say that, so he just promised that he would implore the boy at the end of each school day to go home and crack open his textbooks.

LUNCHTIME. *Elementary school students move their desks into a circle and eat a lunch of Japanese curry and rice.*

SHOULD YOUR CHILD ATTEND A JAPANESE SCHOOL?

If your child is of junior high or high school age with no previous Japanese language background, it would be almost impossible for him to succeed in a Japanese school. The language barrier in both speaking and writing would be extraordinarily difficult to initially overcome, and even then he would constantly be playing catch-up. For parents who find it important for their children to learn the Japanese language, remember that all international schools should offer Japanese language courses, and supplemental instruction could be provided by either language schools or private tutors.

Parents of elementary school students might, however, consider a Japanese school, as the pressures at that level are far less. The most obvious benefits include an alternative learning experience, a solid grounding in a second language, and no need to pay private school tuition. The possible drawback will lie in the quality of your child's teacher; some teachers really do break the mold of rote-memorization and an overemphasis on rules, but some don't.

Obviously, a successful experience for all requires a supportive principal and a talented teacher. If you and your child are interested in this option, visit your local elementary school.

INTERNATIONAL SCHOOLS

There are a number of private international schools in Japan; however, these tend to be concentrated in major cities, particularly Tokyo. The schools usually offer a curriculum that is similar to that of U.S. schools, with a similar school calendar. Some schools in Tokyo to consider include the following:

- The American School in Japan, (0422) 34-5300, **www.asij.ac.jp**
- The British School in Tokyo, (03) 5467-4321, **www.bst.ac.jp**
- Tokyo International School, (03) 5484-1160, **www.tokyois.com**
  You can find a listing of other schools in Tokyo and elsewhere,

together with contact information, at the following sites: **www.tokyowithkids.com/fyi/international_schools.html** and **http://knot.mine.nu/japan/inter.html**.

UNIVERSITIES

Like everything else, there is a pecking order to universities that remains largely unchanged from year to year. The top public school in a particular area is considered No. 1, to be followed by the top private school. And the larger the school, usually the "better" it is.

Foreign students who wish to study for an undergraduate degree at a Japanese university, in addition to completing high school at an accredited institution, must also demonstrate satisfactory competence in Japanese. This is usually accomplished by passing Level 1 of the Japanese Language Proficiency Exam. Graduate students, however, may be exempt from this requirement; check with the department.

Each university administers its own entrance examination. The schedules are jury-rigged so that students are limited in how many universities they can apply for; usually they can plan to apply to one public university and one private university. Universities are limited by the Education Ministry as to how many students they can accept. Once admitted, however, it is still not guaranteed that the student will be able to freely choose his own major. The Education Ministry makes decisions as to how many engineers Japan needs, how many businessmen, and so on, and it exerts its influence by limiting how many students can study a particular subject. I know many, many students who wanted to study English at university—but were shut out because the English department had filled its quota. Most of them wound up majoring in law, which I suppose is evidence enough of the ministry's cruelty.

University courses of study, while not being 100 percent prescribed, definitely offer students few elective options. They also require students to spend a lot more time in class than a Western university might; 30 hours of actual sitting-in-class time is considered typical. That, combined with the fact that many students hold one, two, or more part-time jobs, means that students have very little time left over to do homework and learn things by themselves.

I have taught at some of the lesser universities in Japan, and I can say that many of the students had no business being there—they had neither the skills to succeed nor the desire to compete. Naturally, in Japan, they are allowed to graduate if they attend enough classes. If you land a job at a Japanese university, be alerted that there is pressure to make sure that everybody passes—if they don't, you could be out of work.

I have also taught at one of the allegedly top universities in Japan, and I can attest that virtually all of the students were of the highest caliber. Yet more than one of them told me that they were disappointed in their university education. They expected more participation, more discussion, even more expectations from their teachers, but they didn't find it. Instead, most of their classes were sleep-inducing lectures. They had looked forward to university as being a time of adventurous inquisition, and instead many of them found an utter lack of intellectual stimulation.

Graduate study can be equally arduous, though for different reasons. Graduate students are expected to work closely with their assigned faculty members, supporting him in interfaculty disputes and even allowing him to adopt their research as his own. Moreover, most universities are starved for funds that would help them establish top-notch libraries, let alone perform cutting-edge research. Recent changes by the government require formerly public universities to turn a profit; it is not known whether this will actually improve the quality of their education.

CRAM SCHOOLS

Known as *juku*, cram schools demonstrate that public schools are not doing their job; if they were, why would students have to spend evenings and weekends going to a second school? Cram schools help students prepare for entrance exams into high school or university; the most popular subjects are English and math. Though many students of course hate having to go to a cram school after finishing school in the afternoon, a surprising number of students say they like it. Cram school teachers are notably talented and supportive, and cram school is education without the marches, songs, bullies, and mind-numbing rules of public school. Who wouldn't prefer it?

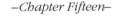

–Chapter Fifteen–

FAMILY ISSUES

"Play is the highest expression of the human development in childhood for it alone is the expression of what is in a child's soul."

–Friedrich Froebel, German originator of kindergarten

Without the bonds of family and social clubs, domestic life can be a bit of a hurdle. Here are some ideas as to what's out there.

Babysitting

It is quite frankly very difficult to find a good student babysitter in Japan. This is because girls and boys, whether in junior high or high school, don't learn how to take care of younger children when they are at that age. Schoolwork thoroughly monopolizes their time, so that in many families teenaged children are not even held accountable for such a simple task as taking out the garbage, let alone minding a young child.

Professional, experienced babysitters are expensive. Many services require registrations and an annual fee. You can get a trial course from Poppins Service in Shibuya-ku at (03) 3447-2100 for between 1,600 and 2,500 yen/hour. You can find a list of other agencies that provide babysitting service at the following website: **www.tokyowithkids.com/babysitters/comm_services.html**.

Day Care

For children who are too young to attend elementary school, there are two options: kindergarten and day care. Unlike many Western kindergartens, which are only for the one year before elementary school, kindergarten (*youchien*) in Japan is for children both four and five years old. The routine is similar to that of other kindergartens around the world: a gentle curriculum of games and basic skills geared for young children. Except for some exclusive private kindergartens, there are no uniforms, although typically children do wear a smock and a yellow cap. The latter is so that they can be easily spotted (and hopefully avoided) by motorists.

Although kindergarten admittance is generally noncompetitive, be aware that some "name" kindergartens — particularly those that are part of a larger education empire that may go all the way through to university — will have entrance exams. Little children are judged by how well they recognize colors, how well they can identify different shapes, and so on. Enough said.

Kindergarten can of course be a good experience in general, but as it usually finishes by 3 p.m., it may not be a realistic option for working parents. The alternative is day care, or nursery school (*hoikuen*), which is open to all children until they are ready for elementary school.

One possible reason for the dearth of children in Japan is that day care can be damn hard to come by. Few companies go out of their way to help working moms, and of course working dads are never thought to be in need of assistance since the care of children is expected to be handled by mothers. The three factors when considering day care are of course quality, price, and convenience. If you've found all three in the same school, count your blessings.

Day care facilities come in three types: government, licensed private, and unlicensed private. Government day care is priced according to the family's income; a boon to low-income families, a headache for higher-income ones. Both government and licensed private day care centers are strictly regulated in many areas, including the teacher-child ratio. The problem, however, is that there are not enough day care centers, particularly of the government variety. Many schools have waiting lists; if you're pregnant now and you anticipate needing day care in the future, by all means get your name down on a list right now.

To fill the gap, there is unlicensed private day care, the most common in Japan. The phrase "unlicensed day care" may surely strike fear into any parent's heart, but actually it can represent both the best and the worst of day care facilities. On the negative side, there is a chain of unlicensed day care centers near my home which had a child in its care die, most likely because the teacher-child ratio was so extreme. On the positive side, it gives day care teachers the freedom to do their jobs as they see fit without burdensome government regulations. After a lot of careful consideration, my wife and I decided to enroll our daughter in an unlicensed day care facility. The head teacher is a remarkably dedicated woman, who oversees a perpetually engaging and stimulating day care program. I'd say more about it myself, but I think the best opinion comes from my own daughter: She loves it.

By contrast, government day care centers may actually be some-what slack. Popular opinion is that such day care teachers don't work as hard as private day care teachers do, simply because their jobs are absolutely guaranteed. While I can't vouch for that, I will say that, after having visited many day care facilities myself, I would offer some advice to parents who are looking for day care in Japan:

- What is the school's reputation—not just its name, but its reputation for taking care of children?
- Do the teachers, and the head teacher in particular, demonstrate a kind attitude? In the process of finding day care I met more than one teacher who put me off with her cold, schoolmarmish attitude.
- Does there seem to be a good teacher-child ratio?
- Does the school offer a wide variety of activities during the year?

Like any other school in Japan, day care will have its share of sports days, culture days, and other activities. Should you enroll your child in day care, if nothing else you'll be impressed at how quickly your child learns Japanese!

MAIDS

Because Japanese homes are relatively small, most people do not have need for a maid. Finding a live-in maid may be particularly difficult. Should you require part-time maid service, however, you can contact the Tokyo Domestic Service Center at (03) 3584-4760. The charge for one day is 12,500 yen.

SPOUSAL EMPLOYMENT

Spouses of full-time employees in Japan who seek employment for themselves should first check to see whether the visa they hold permits paid employment. Without the correct visa no legal employment can be sought. There are openings, however, for private teachers of English and other languages which are paid in cash "under the table". Temporary or one-time employment that is similarly paid exists in other fields; check your local English-language magazine or community bulletin board for openings.

Chapter Sixteen

HEALTH AND
SAFETY

"My doctor grabbed me by the wallet and said, 'Cough!'"
–Comedian Henry Youngman

Like a movie villain who makes his entrance only during the last reel, I have saved one of the darker sides of Japan for the end—its health system. Though there are of course many terrific doctors, dentists, and nurses, there are also too many who are either uncaring or incompetent. I would like to stress that that is not only my opinion— that is also the opinion I have gotten from conversations with the talented health care professionals I have had the opportunity to meet in Japan over the years.

HEALTH CONCERNS

Generally speaking, Japan is a healthy country. There are no outbreaks of diseases common to equatorial countries, such as yellow fever or malaria. The one exotic disease is Japanese encephalitis, a mosquito-borne disease that attacks the brain and has an estimated 30 percent mortality rate. The incidence of this disease is small and is usually limited to a few people raising pigs in Kyushu. For the record, I've spent time around farm animals in Kyushu and have never had any worries, but if you feel that that merely indicates a lack of good judgment on my part, you might wish to consult information provided by the Center for Disease Control at **www.cdc.gov/ncidod/dvbid/ jencephalitis/qa.htm**. A preventive vaccination is available that is good for three years.

Tap water is chlorinated—sometimes too much so—and there shouldn't be any risk of water-borne infections. If you are concerned about pollutants, you might want to consider a water filter for your faucet or a water pitcher with a filter. The air is certainly far cleaner than it was during the industrially polluted '60s, but there can still be bouts of smoggy air. There are also periods of heavy pollination that lead to hay fever and other allergies. One of the unforgivable mistakes of the government was to at one time encourage the widespread planting of Japanese cedar for harvesting. Called *sugi*, this tree can give people a strong allergic reaction from February to April. The story goes that the government will eventually eliminate many *sugi* farms, but only after the trees have been cut and the farmers have pocketed their profits. In the meantime …

March will see the sky in many parts of the country turn orange as the air becomes filled with microscopic grains of sand, carried by the wind from the parts of China that have become subject to desertification. It can be a nuisance when you take your laundry in at night, but it shouldn't cause any problems otherwise. Otherwise, the only other troubles you might experience will be prickly heat rash in the summer and dry skin and chapped lips in the winter.

DRUG STORES

Compared to where you're from, you will probably find drug stores in Japan to be something of a joke. Most people go to hospitals in search of serious medicine. By contrast, drug stores will sell a very limited supply of over-the-counter medicines, all of an extremely weak and therefore safe nature. You will also be able to find a large variety of Chinese-style herbal remedies, and although I am not one to knock the benefits of such medicine, I will say that they will almost certainly not provide you with any scientifically based reassurance. I try to stock up on Western medicines each time I return home; aspirin, acetaminophen (Tylenol), and the like. (I also urge you to check the expiration date before purchasing!)

If you have any personally prescribed medicines, including birth control pills, make sure you bring a note from your doctor in case the boys at customs have a question. Most any medicine for personal consumption should be OK, however. I would also recommend bringing a comprehensive medical encyclopedia with you if you plan to stay for any length of time. That way you can be sure to have a fair understanding of your problem even if the doctor cannot begin to explain it to you.

ALTERNATIVE THERAPIES

Along with the aforementioned herbal medicines, there are other alternatives to Western hospital care. Acupuncture is a highly respected practice which many people find helpful, particularly for joint and muscle pain. The treatment may not provide a permanent cure, but it certainly does provide relief for many patients. Other available treatments include chiropractic and shiatsu massage, a wonderfully therapeutic massage.

Many young Japanese women with money to spend, and some men, will visit an aromatherapy clinic. You can find aromatherapy clinics anywhere these days—they provide a darkened atmosphere, a soothing cup of tea, and restorative music, all to the scent of burning oil touched with different fragrances. All for the right price, of course. Another popular option is reflexology, which is the manipulation of certain pressure points (as identified by Chinese tradition) in order to relieve stress.

Shiatsu massage is a Japanese form of massage that became codified during the last century. Chinese medicine holds that people have energy flowing through different channels throughout their bodies. *Shiatsu* aims to manipulate those channels to relieve pain. There are many massage clinics that practice *shiatsu* and other forms of massage. Some of these, however, are of the dodgy variety; if a clinic only keeps daylight hours, odds are it's a legitimate clinic.

DOCTORS AND HEALTH CLINICS

For initial consultation regarding a malady, all you need to do at a clinic is show up—you virtually never need to make an appointment. Any subsequent visits will require an appointment, which will be made at the end of the previous visit. When you arrive at the clinic, you will have to present your insurance card if you have Japanese medical insurance. You will in all likelihood be issued a small ID card, which you should present upon future visits.

The bad points ... well, where do I begin? For starters, a lot of hospitals that bill themselves in locally prepared publications as being "English friendly!" may not actually be so upon arrival. I chose one hospital based upon its nearness to my office, but also because the city hospital guide said that English was spoken for patients who needed English consultation. As soon as I sat down with the doctor, however, the first words he said were, "Can you speak Japanese?" It turned out that, while he might have been able to speak English, he wasn't inclined to try, and kept answering many of my English questions with Japanese answers.

Many municipalities will publish books with really swell titles like "Directory of English-Speaking Doctors and Hospitals in X City", and many of them are replete with lies. What happens is that it's prestigious for a clinic to be listed as such, so pressure is applied on the publisher ... you get the idea. My advice is to call the clinic first and ask to speak with the doctor in English. If you're not satisfied with a short conversation, you won't have to waste your time on a poor consultation.

Additionally, unless you wind up making an appointment at an obviously posh clinic (easily identified by the cute bric-a-brac decorating a very new building), it is likely that you will not have a separate examination room. I visited one ear, nose, and throat specialist, and I thought I'd accidentally wandered into a queue for army recruits. Two lines of patients led to the doctor seated in the middle, who would gesture for one patient to sit down and prepare himself while he used his swivel chair to whip around and examine the other patient. Having my problems on display for everyone else in the room was not exactly what I'd had in mind.

Why does that happen? It's because all doctors in Japan, whether in the heart of downtown Tokyo or in the sticks of the remotest island, are required by the government to charge exactly the same fee for the same procedure. So the only way that a doctor can rake in the big bucks is by maxing out on the number of patients he sees in one day. That is certainly one reason that a visit to a doctor in Japan can be a cold experience. He's too busy sending you off to get an expensive test done so he can move on to the next patient, rather than taking the time to ask you questions and listen to your answers.

Other problems that you might face:

- An over-prescribing of drugs. Many doctors run clinics which— surprise, surprise!—have some sort of connection with the next-door drug store. Sometimes the doctor himself operates the drug-dispensing pharmacy. Either way, too many doctors wind up prescribing unnecessary antibiotics for viral infections, or worse.
- Incorrect dosages. The prescribed dosage may have no connection as to what is required for optimal treatment. You may have to check your own resources as to what might be the optimal dosage.

- Powdered drugs. Most doctors are unaware that there is at least one domestic manufacturer of a certain drug in pill form. Additionally, since April 2004 government rules make individual hospitals responsible for their own profits and losses, so they have little incentive to recommend pills if they are more expensive. As a consequence, doctors and hospitals continue to prescribe the very annoying powders. If you want pills or capsules, you will have to insist.
- Lack of information. Generally speaking, drug stores will group your medicines into different bags, i.e., the drugs in this bag should be taken once a day, the drugs in that bag should be taken twice a day, etc. There is no information that is provided in Japanese, let alone English, as to the name of the medicine, the size of the dosage, side effects, or any number of routine answers to questions you might have. If that troubles you, get the doctor to answer your questions before you head off to the drug counter.

Nurses may know how to perform routine tasks, or they may not. Too many of them went to nursing school in search of doctor husbands. That may be why many younger nurses seem to have an attitude of "let's get this exam over with" while older ones have more humanity; the older nurses are still there because they are the ones who truly like what they do.

Ambulances have some lifesaving equipment, but ambulance crews are a long way from acting like paramedics in other countries. Many of them have the attitude of "wait until we get to the hospital and the doctor can check you." Of course, some people thus die en route. Many Japanese who have a medical emergency choose to take a taxi to the hospital instead; taxi drivers are probably more aggressive than ambulance drivers, and the patient or his family can choose which hospital to be taken to.

In fairness, I should hasten to express my deep gratitude to those doctors and nurses who have treated me and my family with competence, kindness, and compassion. They are just as talented and as professional as any doctors and nurses in the world. But both they, and I, know that the quality of care they consistently provide should be the norm and not the exception. There is no excuse for the poor level of care that many doctors provide, and constantly get away with, in Japan.

Recommended hospitals in Tokyo include Tokyo Medical and Surgical Clinic in Minato-ku (03) 3436-3028 and the International Clinic Tojinmachi in Fukuoka (090) 3987-6908. You can also find a guide to other hospitals in Japan at the following website: **http:// jguide.stanford.edu/site/hospitals_clinics_2110.html**.

DENTISTS

Dental procedures take far, far too long over here. You may visit a dentist for what you think is a routine, one-shot procedure—only to be told that it will actually take four visits to complete. Of course, sometimes those repeat visits may truly be necessary—but for a filling? If you find yourself needing dental treatment and you feel confident about how many times you should have to see the doctor, you should let your doctor know at the beginning of the consultation. He may strongly advise against it; you will have to use your own judgment regarding the matter.

Most dentists give their patients acrylic fillings, rather than silver fillings, primarily because the acrylic fillings can be domestically produced. However, techniques that are being developed in other countries to treat oral problems have been slow to be adopted in Japan.

Perhaps the most irresponsible move taken by dentists as a whole, however, is the way the Japan Dental Association has constantly fought against the fluoridation of its public water supply. One U.S. dentist whose career straddled both sides of the fluoridation divide said that before it was rare to find a child who didn't have any cavities, but after it was rare to find the child who did. Dentists in such advanced countries didn't get in the way of public health; instead, they found other ways to maintain their standard of living. In Japan, however, dentists seem more intent on preserving their cash cows—their cavity-prone patients—rather than doing the right thing and supporting an all-too-obvious public health measure.

HEALTH INSURANCE

If you are a full-time employee (*seishain*) of a company or institution, your employer should offer you the opportunity to join the *shakai hoken*, which is a health insurance plan scheme for salaried workers. Self-employed workers who want similar insurance must obtain the *kokumin hoken*. It is possible to purchase the health insurance without joining the government's accompanying pension plans; however, you cannot join the pension plan without getting the health insurance as well.

Although the co-payment is reasonable (currently 30 percent), the monthly premiums are indexed according to your salary and can be incredibly expensive. Plus, if you reside in a certain area for a couple of years without the insurance and then decide later on to join, you will have to make back payments dating to the time you first moved in. (Ouch!) Once you join, there is no legal way you can get off the plan except by moving to a new locality, in which case you would have to re-register if you wanted to join the plan again.

My feeling is that, if your employer obligates you to join the national insurance plan, of course you must accept it. Otherwise, check into overseas medical insurance as it will be far, far cheaper. Countries like Britain and New Zealand have insurance companies with long experience in dealing with expatriate claims. You will, of course, have to pay the bill in full yourself at a Japanese clinic and await reimbursement from your insurance company later. You will also have to deal with the quizzical looks from Japanese hospital staff, who may never have encountered non-Japanese insurance before. But it certainly tops paying into Japan's system, the premiums of which can increase at a bureaucrat's whim.

CRIME AND SAFETY

Is Japan a safe country? I don't know—why don't you ask all of the commuters who fall asleep next to complete strangers on the trains?

Japan has to be safe; a cash-based society could not be otherwise. One can walk down the streets of most any city in Japan and feel safer day or night than in any other comparably-sized city in the world. And while people are not averse to stealing cash out of neglected wallets, it is still possible that the empty wallet will be turned in.

Still, to say that the crime rate, including the rate of violent crime, is less than that of your own country does not mean it is zero, either. The most common sort of crime these days seems to be robbery. Criminals seem to be particularly adept at entering apartments through balcony windows, even those apartments that are several floors off the ground. The most common targets of theft are cash and—I'm not joking—women's underwear. Many robbery attempts have taken place while people were actually in the apartment at the time, no matter the time of day.

If you need a police officer, the emergency number for calling the police is 110. Or, you can visit the nearest police box. Police boxes are conveniently located throughout Japan, and likely as not you will see some police officer there seated ramrod-straight at his desk, just waiting for the criminals to enter and turn themselves in. What you will not see in Japan, however, are police officers on patrol throughout the neighborhood, possibly deterring criminals through their simple presence. There is a strong suspicion that the *reported* crime rate in Japan is low simply because the police take care to avoid witnessing crimes in the first place.

If there is another problem with safety in Japan, it lies in the atrocious design of its architecture and public works. Granted that the Japanese are a historically small people living in a crowded country, it is still difficult to explain why venturing forth into public has to be so dangerous. Covered concrete gutters along the road will suddenly become uncovered. Overhangs will crack the head of the unwary

233

pedestrian. And blind corners are everywhere.

Moreover, what is truly criminal is the attitude of the public agencies whose job is to oversee companies' compliance with the regulations of Japan. Any public agency that plans an inspection will usually take the courtesy of telephoning and announcing its intention beforehand, thereby giving the company enough time to make good its violations. I worked for one company that took down its room dividers in time for the fire marshal's inspection and then put them back up afterwards. And I know a department store that uses its wide stairs for box storage, leaving only enough space for people to pass single file. The fires at substandard clubs that take people's lives, the dairy companies that carelessly permit widespread food poisoning, and the industrial firms that disgorge untreated pollutants into the water are all symptoms of a government that really can't be bothered about taking care of its people. Public safety? In Japan it's a joke.

Chapter Seventeen

SETTLING DOWN
IN JAPAN

"It is possible, but not at the moment."
–The doorkeeper's answer to the man seeking the Law
in *Before the Law* by Franz Kafka

Processing the correct documents in Japan can be like a comedy routine at times. To wit: I know a Canadian woman who, while on holiday in New Zealand, lost her passport. She promptly got a new passport from the Canadian embassy in Auckland, but she also needed to get a new working visa to resume her job in Japan. So she contacted her boss in Japan, who offered to go to the government office in the ward where she lived and get the document that would establish her proof of residence, which in turn would enable her to get a new visa.

The helpful young man at the ward office prepared all of the documents necessary for her to get her visa—but there was a catch. He could only release all of the relevant documents if the Canadian woman could sign for them.

"But she's in New Zealand and can't come back here unless she has the visa," said her boss.

"Well, I'm very sorry, but I need her signature before you can take the documents," the official answered.

Back and forth they went, but they were no closer to a solution. Totally at an impasse, the woman's boss asked if there was any way out of the situation.

"Well," said the official, "you could sign her name for her."

There was the answer. A government official was openly advising someone to break out of the rules-imposed box by committing what would be considered a major crime in many Western countries, merely for the sake of having his own paperwork tidily in order.

VISAS

Hopefully, most short-time visitors to Japan won't have to deal with such Kafkaesque officials. Tourists from many countries are granted a 90-day tourist visa upon arrival; for travelers from other countries, a visa is required, but it is not too terribly difficult to secure. The government has announced its goal of dramatically increasing tourism in the near future, so it would be unlikely that Japan would make it more difficult for people to visit.

People who are in Japan to work must obtain the correct working visa. This must be obtained before you enter the country; if you find work while in Japan on a tourist visa, you will have to leave the country and re-enter on your working visa. For many foreigners, this is what South Korea is for. However, if you constantly travel back and forth between the two countries, you will find your passport and effects scrutinized more thoroughly than they perhaps otherwise might be.

Along with your visa application you should submit a certificate of eligibility. The certificate of eligibility shows that you qualify for the visa that you seek. If you seek a work visa, for example, you will have to document that your employer will provide you with a minimum income. The qualification for this employee sponsorship is normally 250,000 yen/month (3 million yen/year), but exceptions may be made. If you do not work full-time for one employer but work part-time for several, you can sponsor yourself. You will have to obtain documentation from each of your part-time employers to show that you will make the minimum annual salary.

If you marry a Japanese person, you are eligible for a spousal visa, which permits you to reside and work in Japan. These visas, however, will receive tighter scrutiny than the others, and you may find yourself having to renew your visa after three months initially. If you are married for three years, or continuously employed with one Japanese firm for ten years, you are eligible for a permanent resident visa. These visas are easier to get than they used to be, and they are required before one can purchase property in Japan.

There are other visas available, most of which do not permit employment. An exception is the working holiday visa, available to citizens of those countries that have reciprocal agreements with Japan. Work under such permits is limited to 20 hours of employment a week. For more information about visas, check the website provided by the Ministry of Foreign Affairs at **www.mofa.go.jp/j_info/visit/ visa/index.html**.

Non-tourist visa holders must obtain a re-entry visa before traveling abroad. The visas can be good for up to three years; you have your choice of getting a single-entry visa for 3,000 yen or a multiple-entry visa for 6,000 yen. Unless you have a sincere desire to hang out with the gang at immigration as much as possible, I suggest you avoid the paperwork and the hassle and get the multiple-entry visa.

Non-Japanese who enter on anything other than a tourist visa must also apply for a card known as the *gaikokujin tourokusho* and known to most resident foreigners as their "gaijin card". It can be obtained from the ward office or city or town hall in the area where you live. You will need one passport-sized photograph. It is strongly requested that you appear at that office within two weeks of entering the country on your visa. If you renew your visa, move to a different location, or change to a new visa, you should again square away the details at the appropriate office within two weeks.

Note that in the wake of the terrorist attacks of September 11, 2001 in the United States, overstaying a visa is now considered a crime in Japan.

OTHER USEFUL DOCUMENTS

An international driver's license, together with a driver's license issued in your home country, is immensely useful if you plan to go driving anywhere. Be aware that an international driver's license is only valid for your first year of residence—after that, you are expected to apply for a Japanese driver's license should you wish to continue driving. To apply for a Japanese driver's license, you will first have to visit a branch of the Japan Automobile Federation (**www.jaf.or.jp/e/index_e.htm**) to obtain a document stating that the license issued in your home country was issued three months before entering the country. (And if you wind up getting a new driver's license in your home country after entering Japan but before applying for a Japanese license, as I did, you're going to have to ask the motor vehicle administration in your state or country to issue a Photostat of a previous license!) Then you will have to go to the nearest driver's license center and take a written test. Some nationalities will also be required to take a driving test; others won't.

You can only obtain a license for a vehicle equivalent to the one that you drove at home; if you didn't have a motorcycle license before, you can't get licensed for one in Japan without going through an absurdly expensive Japanese driving school.

A university transcript will be necessary for many jobs. Some employers may say that a university transcript is not sufficient proof of your university degree and demand a photocopy of the actual degree itself. It's up to you as to whether you want to bring it with you; mine continues to sit in its frame on the wall in my parents' house and hasn't come out yet.

CUSTOMS

Visitors to Japan can bring up to three bottles of alcohol, 100 cigars, 400 cigarettes, and 2 ounces of perfume with them duty-free. They can also bring 100 kg of rice per year into the country. Personal effects are of course duty-free, and household effects for those who will stay more than one year are also duty-free, even including automobiles, providing all the paperwork is in order. Other goods of a value greater than 300,000 yen are subject to the appropriate duty. For more information, go to **www.customs.go.jp/zeikan/pamphlet/tsukan_e/top.htm**.

CULTURE QUIZ

HERE'S THE FIRST QUESTION,
STRAIGHT ANSWERS ARE
REQUIRED

TRIGG

SITUATION 1

You are working at your office on Friday afternoon when your boss suddenly announces that there will be a company party this evening after five o'clock. You, however, have already made plans to meet with your own friends at the same time. What is the best option?

A Call your friends and cancel your plans with them.
B Respectfully tell your boss that you cannot attend the company party.
C Try to divide your time between your office party and your friends' party.
D Sit at your desk and quietly moan about how people in Japan will spring things on you at the last moment.

The answer is, like so many other things in Japan, "It all depends." **A** is probably the best choice under most circumstances, as friends can be very sympathetic about such obligations—certainly more sympathetic than most bosses. **B**, however, might be acceptable in some circumstances, for example, if your friends are very dear and you won't see them again for a long time, or if your company has had a rash of parties recently, and there will be future opportunities to make up for it later. **C** is probably the worst choice, all things considered; if you're going to attend a party, it's best to stay until it has officially ended, rather than split your time between the two. Of course, **D** is a perfectly acceptable thing to do as well, but by itself it doesn't get the problem solved!

SITUATION 2

For what seems like the 17th time in two days, someone compliments you on your ability to use chopsticks by saying, "*Ohashi wa jouzu desu ne!*" How should you respond?

A Show your appreciation and your wacky sense of humor by fixing the chopsticks under your upper lip like walrus tusks.

B Secretly express your irritation by picking up a piece of soy sauce-coated raw fish, then "accidentally" flicking it in his lap.

C Sarcastically gush every time he successfully feeds himself with a fork.

D Thoroughly abase yourself by commenting on how bad you really are and how much more practice you truly need.

While **A** might be considered quality humor at a ribald drinking party, it is neither good manners nor an adequate answer. **B** is of course a reprehensible example of internationalization. **C** is also a poor choice, and probably a sign that you're not dealing well with living in Japan anymore. **D** is the only correct choice, as it would be considered extremely polite to refuse the compliment and instead belittle one's abilities by saying something like, "*Iie – mada mada desu.*" ("Nah – I'm still practicing.")

SITUATION 3

While on vacation, you have selected some souvenirs for a couple of the really nice people at your office, but you have neither the means nor the desire to buy the same souvenirs for the other 31 people in your section. What can you do?

A Make an ostentatious display of presenting the gifts to the people you like while thoroughly ignoring everyone else.

B Give everyone a small present of either stale cookies or mysterious seafood.

C Buy 31 more of the expensive souvenirs and charge them to your credit card in the knowledge that it is terrifically important to maintain company *wa*, no matter how great the personal expense.

D Regretfully return all of the souvenirs you chose for your friends back to the shelf; after all, presents lose their value if people are always expecting them.

Perhaps surprisingly, **B** is the best choice. It really doesn't matter what kind of gifts you give so long as you give something. Later, you can also give the nice souvenirs to your friends when no one else is looking. **A**, on the other hand, is the worst choice as odds are you will truly rub someone the wrong way with your selective kindness. **D** is almost as bad, as there are some people who will wonder why you are so selfish as to forget them while you're on holiday having a good time. **C**, although a generous proposition from your colleagues' point of view, certainly doesn't do you any good. Although complete selflessness is an admirable trait in Japan, remember that you've got to take care of yourself as well.

SITUATION 4

Moments before immersing yourself in a demanding new task, your friend pulls you aside and exhorts, "Do your best!" How can you best answer him?

A Snap that you always do your best, and it's pretty insulting for him to suggest otherwise.

B Confound everyone's expectations and immediately proceed to do your worst, thereby blowing it.

C Stand there open-mouthed without saying a thing in return.

D Thank him, because you recognize that his English education must have been severely lacking and that he really intended to wish you good luck.

The best choice would be **D**. While it's true that many people have not grasped the nuances of English, this instance is certainly more understandable than others; "Do your best!" is a reasonably direct translation of the Japanese, "*Gambatte!*", which is what all Japanese say to each other before working hard. Both **A** and **B** are self-defeating, particularly so since your friend's intentions were entirely kind and sympathetic. **C** is merely what I did the first time it happened to me.

SITUATION 5

Mr. Tanaka is retiring today at the grand old age of 59 $\frac{1}{2}$, and you've wrestled with your English–Japanese dictionary for a full five minutes trying to come up with the correct Japanese phrase for the occasion. Translated into English, that phrase would be:

A "Congratulations!"

B "You must be tired."

C "Don't let the *fusuma* hit you on the way out!"

D "Uh, about your pension …"

Surprisingly, **A** is *not* the correct choice. For many men this is not a valedictory moment, but rather the severing of the most important connection in their lives. **C** is not a witty adaptation of an English phrase but instead something that would leave everyone puzzled. **D** becomes more truthful with each passing year, but it's not exactly relevant to the moment. The correct choice would be **B**. (See the Glossary to find that phrase in Japanese. And yes, I've gotten this one wrong myself, too.)

SITUATION 6

Your host has just placed a beautifully arranged lunch of rice, *wakame* soup, broiled fish, and cabbage before you. You love fish, you can take or leave the cabbage, you're allergic to the sesame seeds in the soup, and if you have one more bowlful of sticky white rice you're just going to be sick. Nevertheless, to impress your host you should begin by eating:

A The soup
B The rice
C The fish
D The cabbage

The correct answer is, "It doesn't really matter." Yes, there are many more rules in Japan for the simplest activities than you have probably come to expect in your own country. But there is also a tendency among some foreigners to get carried away with internalizing too many guidelines. There are still a million situations in Japan for which there are no hard and fast rules. If by chance you do end up transgressing an unwritten law, well, the Japanese can be very forgiving of your lack of knowledge.

DOS AND DON'TS

What follows is a quick laundry list of basic tips to surviving in Japan.

- **Do** take off your shoes before stepping up into a house, or into some schools and restaurants, and then put on the slippers provided.
- **Don't** walk on Japanese straw mats (*tatami*) while wearing your slippers—take them off.
- **Do** change into the toilet slippers when using the bathroom. (But **don't** forget to change out of them when leaving the toilet!)
- **Don't** stick your chopsticks into your rice bowl or pass food with your chopsticks. Both of these things are only done at funerals.
- **Do** wash and rinse yourself completely before slipping into a Japanese bath.
- **Do** try to learn the basics of the Japanese writing system, i.e., *hiragana* and *katakana*, as well as learn how to write your address in Japanese.
- **Do** address people by their surnames and correct title, e.g., Tanaka-*san*. Remember that it is rude and embarrassing to use given names in public situations, even among very good friends.
- **Don't** expect Japan to change for you while you live there. Likewise, **don't** give up suggesting change that is fair and equitable for all.
- **Do** remember that, fairly or not, your country and compatriots will be judged based on how you behave.
- **Do** keep in mind that an individual Japanese person is no more responsible for the whole of his culture than you are of yours—so **don't** always be asking, "Why?"
- **Don't** be shocked or offended by people's behavior when drunk (unless they are really over the line).
- **Do** be patient.

GLOSSARY

BASIC JAPANESE PHRASES

Some of these appeared in other sections, but I have grouped them here for easy consultation.

- *Arigatou gozaimasu* –Polite way to say "thank you". If it's the last thank-you of a particular transaction, can be changed to *arigatou gozaimashita*.
- *Doumo*–Equivalent to saying "thanks" for a minor task, such as when someone pours your drink. Can also be a casual greeting.
- *Douzo*– "Please," as in the sense of "Please accept this drink" or "Please go before me."
- *Onegai shimasu*– "Please", as in the sense of "If you don't mind." Useful for getting a clerk's attention.
- *Kudasai*– "Please," as in the sense of "please give me something." "*Mizu kudasai*"–"Water, please."
- *Sumimasen*–"Excuse me" as either apology or attention-getter.
- *Gomen nasai*–"I'm sorry." Connotes very personal regret.
- *Ojama shimasu*–"Excuse me." Used when entering another's home.
- *Shitsurei shimasu*– "Excuse me," in the sense of joining or leaving a group. Also used to end a telephone conversation.
- *Moshi moshi*–Used to begin a telephone conversation.
- *Osaki ni douzo*–"After you."
- *Yoroshiku onegai shimasu*– "Please take care of me." The best words with which to begin a relationship. Can be simply *yoroshiku* in a casual setting.
- *Omedetou gozaimasu*–"Congratulations!"
- *Go-shuushou-sama desu*–"I'm sorry." For funeral condolences only.

- *Ittekimasu*–"I'm going." Used when leaving home in the morning, or when leaving work on an errand.
- *Itterashai*–"Go and come back." The correct response to *ittekimasu*.
- *Tadaima*–"I'm back." Said upon one's return.
- *O-kaeri nasai*–"Welcome back." The proper response to *tadaima*.
- *Osaki ni shitsurei shimasu*–"I'm leaving." Said when departing the office for the day.
- *Otsukare-sama deshita*–"You must be tired." The proper response to *osaki ni shitsurei shimasu*.
- *Ohayou gozaimasu*–"Good morning." Used until that point in the morning when you start to feel hungry for lunch, or when starting the work shift at any time.
- *Konnichiwa*–"Good afternoon." Used until dusk.
- *Kombanwa*–"Good evening." Used after dusk.
- *Oyasumi nasai*–"Good night." Used when going to bed.
- *Sayounara*–"Goodbye." Used far less than one might first imagine. It implies a certain finality that this is truly goodbye.
- *Hai*–"Yes." Also an all-purpose word of acknowledgement.
- *Iie*– "No." Used much less frequently, relatively speaking, than *hai*, which is not surprising in a society where people want to look agreeable.
- … *ne?*–"Right?" A tag at the end of sentences when the speaker is looking for agreement.
- *So desu ne*–"Yes, that's right."
- *Chigaimasu*–"No, that's incorrect."
- *Chotto matte kudasai*–"Just a moment, please."
- *Omatase shimashita*–"Sorry to keep you waiting." Should the waiting be truly excessive, can be changed to *taihen omatase shimashita*.
- *Ikura desu ka*–"How much is it?"
- *Go-yukkuri douzo*–"Please take your time." Spoken when you want your guests to relax and enjoy the meal.
- *Betsu betsu*–"Separately," such as when splitting a dinner bill.

- *Issho*–"Together," such as when paying or doing something together.
- *Toire wa doko desu ka*–"Where is the toilet?"
- *Abunai!*–"It's dangerous!"
- *Tetsudatte*–"Please help me with this task."
- *Tasukete!*–"Help!"
- *Hidari/migi ni magatte kudasai*–"Please turn left/right."
- *Massugu itte kudasai*–"Please go straight."
- *Koko de ii desu*–"Here is fine."
- *~ wa doko desu ka*– "Where is ~ ?"
- *Nani?*–"What?"
- *Nan desu ka?*–"What is it?"
- *Doushite?*–"Why?"
- *Wakarimasen*–"I don't understand."
- *Shirimasen*–"I don't know."
- *Nihongo wa wakarimasen*–"I don't understand Japanese."
- *Eigo o hanasemasu ka?*– "Can you speak English?"

BASIC KANJI AND KANA

- 入口 (*iriguchi*) – entrance
- 出口 (*deguchi*) – exit
- 非常口 (*hijouguchi*) – emergency exit
- 男 (*otoko*) – man
- 女 (*onna*) – woman
- お手洗い (*otearai*) and トイレ (*toire*) – toilet
- 名前 (*namae*) – name
- 住所 (*juusho*) – address
- 才 (*sai*) – years old
- 駅 (*eki*) – station
- 空港 (*kuukou*) – airport
- 銀行 (*ginkou*) – bank

CALENDAR OF FESTIVALS AND HOLIDAYS

PUBLIC HOLIDAYS

New Year's Day (*Ganjitsu*)	1 January
Coming of Age Day (*Seijin no Hi*)	Second Monday in January
Foundation Day (*Kenkoku Kinen no Hi*)	11 February
Vernal Equinox Day (*Shunbun no Hi*)	20 or 21 March
Green Day (*Midori no Hi*)	29 April
Constitution Day (*Kempo Kinen Bi*)	3 May
"Connecting Holiday"	4 May
Children's Day (*Kodomo no Hi*)	5 May
Marine Day (*Umi no Hi*)	Third Monday in July
Respect for the Aged Day (*Keirou no Hi*)	Third Monday in September
Autumnal Equinox Day (*Shuubun no Hi*)	22 or 23 September
Sports Day (*Taiiku no Hi*)	Second Monday in October
Culture Day (*Bunka no Hi*)	3 November
Labor Thanksgiving Day (*Kinrou Kansha no Hi*)	23 November
Emperor's Birthday (*Tennou Tanjoubi*)	23 December

OTHER HOLIDAYS OF NOTE

Traditional New Year's Day (*Koshougatsu*)	15 January
Seasonal Division Day (*Setsubun*)	3 or 4 February
Winter Festival (*Yuki Matsuri*)	5-11 February (Hokkaido)
Valentine's Day	14 February
Doll Festival (*Hina Matsuri*)	3 March
White Day	14 March
Buddha's Birthday/Flower Festival (*Hana Matsuri*)	8 April
Mother's Day	Second Sunday in May
Father's Day	Third Sunday in June
Star Festival (*Tanabata*)	7 July
Festival of the Dead (*O-bon*)	13-15 July (Tokyo)
Festival of the Dead (*O-bon*)	13-15 August (Nationwide)
Seven-Five-Three (*Shichi-Go-San*)	15 November
Christmas Eve	24 December
Christmas Day	25 December
New Year's Holidays (*O-shougatsu*)	29 December–3 January

YEARS

Years are numbered according to both the Gregorian calendar and an emperor's reign. Thus, the year Heisei 16 is the year 2004 in the West. To quickly convert, just keep in mind the years 1925 for Showa (Hirohito) and 1988 for Heisei (Akihito). Thus, someone born in 1977 was born in Showa 52 ('77 minus '25 equals 52), while someone married in 2000 was married in Heisei 12 ('00 minus '88 equals 12).

RESOURCE GUIDE

SERVICE TELEPHONE NUMBERS
- Ambulance – 119
- Fire Department – 119
- Information – 104
- Police – 110
- Time – 117
- Weather – 177

REAL ESTATE AGENCIES
- Century 21 (Tokyo) – **www.century21japan.com** – (03) 3585-0021
- Kencorp (Tokyo) – **www.kencorp.com** – (03) 5413-5666
- Sakura House (Tokyo) – **www.sakura-house.com** – (03) 5330-5250
- Shioya Tochi Co., Ltd. (Kobe) – **www.shioyatochi.co.jp**

MOVING COMPANIES

- Economove Japan Co., Ltd. – **www.economovejapan.com**
- Nihon System Service Co., Ltd. – tel: (0120) 14-0901 [Tokyo], (0120) 29-1200 [Osaka]
- Pakmail – **www.pakmail.co.jp**

TAX AND LAW FIRMS

- Ernst and Young – **www.ey.com/global/content.nsf/Japan_JBS Family_Home**
- KPMG – **http://kpmg.or.jp/english.html**
- Deloitte Touche Tohmatsu – **www.tohmatsu.co.jp/english index.htm/**
- Millbank, Tweed, Hadley, and McCoy LLP (Tokyo) – (03) 3504-2162

A further listing of legal firms in Japan can be found at **www.legal500.com/as500/ja_atoz.htm**.

EMPLOYMENT AGENCIES FOR FOREIGNERS

- Manpower – www.manpower.co.jp/frame_e.html
- Daijob.com – www.daijob.com

Probably the best resource for jobs would be the classified job listings in the English-language magazines and newspapers, particularly the *Japan Times*. There is a nationwide employment agency called "Hello Work", but from all accounts its name belongs to the same class as "Peacekeeping Missiles" or "Military Intelligence"—its fraudulent friendliness is meant to hide the fact that it is not especially helpful. Moreover, the jobs it usually has available are typically scutwork opportunities and that's all.

INTERNATIONAL SCHOOLS

- American School in Japan – (0422) 34-5300

- British School in Tokyo – **www.bst.ac.jp/**
- Canadian International School (Tokyo)
  – **http://61.204.109.177/en/index.asp**
- New International School (Tokyo)
  – **http://newinternationalschool.com**
- Montessori School of Tokyo – (03) 5765-7655
- Osaka International School – **www.senri.ed.jp/**
- Kyoto International School
  – **http://web.kyoto-inet.or.jp/people/hellokis/**
- Fukuoka International School
  – **http://home.att.ne.jp/gamma/fis/index.html**

JAPANESE LANGUAGE SCHOOLS

Probably the most popular Japanese language classes are those taught by the YMCA and YWCA. The YMCA has a convenient site detailing courses taught throughout the country at **http://www.ymcajapan.org/japanese/index.htm**. YWCA courses can be found at individual YWCA sites, such as YWCA Nagoya, etc. For information about other schools, try **www.murasakishikibu.co.jp/jls/**

CULTURAL AND SOCIAL CLUBS

- Tokyo American Club – **www.tac-club.org/**
- The British Club – (03) 3401-1121 and (03) 3401-3691 [Tokyo]; (06) 6449-1411 [Osaka]
- Foreign Executive Women – **www.fewjapan.com**

SPORTS GYMS

Known as sports clubs, there are a few chains that are found throughout the country, including Konami, Renaissance, and NAS. In addition, the major hotel chains (Nikko, ANA, and Hyatt) in the larger cities will also have sports club facilities.

INTERNATIONAL RELIGIOUS INSTITUTIONS

- Synagogues – **http://amyisrael.co.il/asia/japan/**
- Roman Catholic Church
    – **http://home.att.net/~Local_Catholic/Catholic-Japan.htm**
- Baptist Church – **www.tokyobaptist.org/**
- Mosques – **www.ic.u-tokyo.ac.jp/~tuics/Japan/Mosque/**

VOLUNTEER ORGANIZATIONS

- Japanese Red Cross Society – **www.jrc.or.jp/english/index.html**
- Greenpeace Japan – **www.greenpeace.or.jp/index_en_html**
- Amnesty International Japan
    – **www.amnesty.or.jp/** (Japanese only)
- Guardian Angels – **www.guardianangels.or.jp/eng/**

I've already mentioned some good Internet sites in the relevant chapters. Some other excellent websites are as follows:

- **Tokyo English Life Line.** Since 1973, the Tokyo English Life Line continues to take calls from expatriates who are looking for help with a particular problem—or who simply need someone to talk to. This wonderful service can be reached at (03) 5774-0992 or you can visit their website at **www.telljp.com/contact.html**.
- **The Quirky Japan Home Page.** You can find wonderful tidbits about Japanese pop culture here: **www3.tky.3web.ne.jp/~edjacob index.html**.
- **Tokyo Meltdown.** This site is a guide to going out in Tokyo, whether you're looking for restaurants, entertainment, or shopping. It's located at **www.bento.com/tleisure.html**.
- **Japan Today** provides a look at all the breaking news in the country. A good resource. Visit **www.japantoday.com/e ?content=home**.
- **Issho** (a Japanese word meaning "together") is a wonderful site

dedicated to raising attention to those matters that often get swept under the rug in Japan, including labor and women's issues. Visit **www.issho.org/** to see for yourself.

- **The Children's Rights Council Japan** devotes itself to the heartbreaking issues of divorce and child abduction. Divorce in Japan often means that one parent—inevitably the foreigner— will never see his or her child ever afterwards. The CRC fights for parents to have equivalent rights of visitation. Found at **http:/ crcjapan.com/**, the site deserves support.

- **The Japan Telephone Directory** provides yellow page listings for the entire country at **http://english.itp.ne.jp/**.

- Travel information can be found at the website for the **Japan National Tourist Organization** (**www.jnto.go.jp/**). For rail information, check out the **Japan Railways Group** at **www.japanrail.com/**. For airport information, try **Discover Japan** at **www.discover-japan.info/japan_airports.htm**.

FURTHER READING

I'd like to recommend *Culture Shock! Tokyo* by Yuko Morimoto-Yoshida (Times Books International, 2003), for those who enjoyed this book but would like a closer look at living in Tokyo itself. Further recommendations of mine are as follows:

HISTORY

Downfall by Richard B. Frank (Random House, 1999)
Embracing Defeat by John Dower (W.W. Norton, 1999)
Hiroshima by John Hersey (Vintage Books, 1989)
Japan: The Story of a Nation by Edwin O. Reischauer (Tuttle, 1981)
Japan: A Concise History by Milton W. Meyer (Littlefield Adams, 1993)
The Pacific War (Atlantic Communications, 1981)

BIOGRAPHY

American Caesar: Douglas MacArthur 1880–1964 by William Manchester (Little, Brown, 1978)
Hirohito: Behind the Myth by Edward Behr (Vintage, 1989)
My Life Between Japan and America by Edwin O. Reischauer (Harper & Row, 1986)

POLICY

The Enigma of Japanese Power by Karel van Wolferen (Tuttle, 1993)
The Japan That Can Say No by Shintaro Ishihara (Simon and Schuster, 1991)
Japan Versus the West: Image and Reality by Endymion Wilkinson (Penguin, 1990)

Japan: Who Governs? The Rise of the Developmental State by Chalmers Johnson (W.W. Norton, 1995)

SOCIETY

About Face: How I Stumbled Onto Japan's Social Revolution by Clayton Naff (Kodansha, 1994)

The Anatomy of Dependence by Doi Takeo (Kodansha, 1973)

The Chrysanthemum and the Sword by Ruth Benedict (Houghton Mifflin, 1989)

Dogs and Demons: The Fall of Modern Japan by Alex Kerr (Penguin, 2001)

Glimpses of Unfamiliar Japan by Lafcadio Hearn (Tuttle, 1976)

The Japanese Today: Change and Continuity by Edwin O. Reischauer (Belknap, 1988)

The Land of the Rising Yen by George Mikes (Penguin, 1970)

Lost Japan by Alex Kerr (Lonely Planet, 1996)

Pictures From the Water Trade: An Englishman in Japan by John David Morley (Flamingo, 1986)

Straitjacket Society by Miyamoto Masao (Kodansha, 1993)

Thirty-Six Views of Mount Fuji by Cathy N. Davidson (Dutton, 1993)

BUSINESS

The Bubble Economy by Christopher Wood (Tuttle, 1993)

Japan as Number One by Ezra O. Vogel (Harvard University Press, 1979)

Japan Company Handbook Vols. 1 & 2 (Toyo Keizai)

The Reckoning by David Halberstam (Bantam, 1987)

Saving the Sun by Gillian Tett (HarperCollins, 2003)

Turnaround: How Carlos Ghosn Rescued Nissan by David Magee (HarperCollins, 2003)

ARTS AND CULTURE

A Hundred Years of Japanese Film by Donald Richie (Kodansha, 2001)

Appreciations of Japanese Culture by Donald Keene (Kodansha, 1971)

A Book of Five Rings by Miyamoto Musashi (Overlook, 1974)

The Book of Tea by Okakura Kakuzo (Tuttle, 1956)

The Couch Potato's Guide to Japan: Inside the World of Japanese TV by Wm. Penn [Kathleen Morikawa] (Forest River Press, 2003)

Japanese Literature Reviewed by Donald Richie (ICG Muse, 2003)

Japan: A Short Cultural History by G.B. Sansom (Tuttle, 1973)

The Meaning of Ichiro: The New Wave From Japan and the Transformation of Our National Pastime by Robert Whiting (Warner, 2004)

TRAVEL

Gateway to Japan (Kodansha, 1998)

Hiking in Japan: An Adventurer's Guide to the Mountain Trails by Paul Hunt (Kodansha, 1988)

Ski Japan! by T.R. Reid (Kodansha, 1994)

LANGUAGE STUDY

The Complete Japanese Verb Guide by the Hiroo Japanese Center (Tuttle, 1989)

Gone Fishin': New Angles on Perennial Problems by Jay Rubin (Kodansha, 1992)

A Guide to Writing Kanji and Kana Books I & II by Wolfgang Hadamitzky and Mark Spahn (Tuttle, 1991)

Kanji and Kana by Wolfgang Hadamitzky and Mark Spahn (Tuttle, 1981)

Japanese for Everyone by Nagara Susumu, et al (Gakken, 1990)

Japanese for Everyone Workbook (Gakken, 1994)

Japanese-English Dictionary by Shimizu Mamoru and Narita
  Shigehisa (Kodansha, 1979)
Making Out in Japanese by Todd and Erika Geers (Tuttle, 2003)
The Practical English-Japanese Dictionary by Noah S. Brannen
  (Weatherhill, 1991)
Tuttle Kanji Cards by Alexander Kask (Tuttle, 1995)

EDUCATION

Educating Andy by Anne and Andy Conduit (Kodansha, 1996)
"English Heritage" by P. Sean Bramble (*The New Republic*, 17 March
  2003)
Japanese Higher Education as Myth by Brian J. McVeigh (M.E.
  Sharpe, 2002)

FICTION

There's a lot of good fiction out there worth reading. In the interests
of saving space, however, I will mention only those books or writers
that, for different reasons, you should probably have some familiarity
with: Murasaki's *Tale of Genji*, Michael Crichton's *Rising Sun*,
Natsume Soseki's *Botchan* and *I Am a Cat*, James Clavell's *Shogun*,
Yoshikawa Eiji's *Musashi*, and anything by Mishima Yukio, Kawabata
Yasunari, Yoshimoto Banana, and Murakami Haruki.

ABOUT THE AUTHOR

 P. Sean Bramble was born in Cambridge, Maryland, and grew up there and in La Cañada-Flintridge, California. After graduating from The Johns Hopkins University in Baltimore with a degree from the Writing Seminars department, he wrote for two Maryland newspapers, *The Daily Banner* and *The Daily Times*, and a computer newsletter, *The Report on IBM*. Moving to Japan courtesy of the JET Program in 1992, he has taught English there ever since, apart from a stint teaching in Shanghai, China. Stricken with writer's block for approximately 10 years, he has so far managed to overcome it with occasional pieces, including commentary for *The New Republic*. *Culture Shock! Japan* is his first book.

Mr. Bramble lives in Dazaifu, Japan, with his wife and daughter.

INDEX